AIRLINES AT WAR

BRITISH CIVIL AVIATION

1939 - 1944

AIRLINES AT WAR

BRITISH CIVIL AVIATION

1939 - 1944

AN OFFICAL HISTORY

AIR WORLD

AIR WORLD

AIRLINES AT WAR
British Civil Aviation 1939 - 1944

This edition published in 2018 by Air World Books,
an imprint of Pen & Sword Books Ltd,
47 Church Street, Barnsley, S. Yorkshire, S70 2AS

First published as *Merchant Airmen: The Air Ministry Account of British Civil Aviation, 1939-1944*, by HMSO, London, 1946.

Text alterations and additions Copyright © Air World Books, 2018

ISBN: 978-1-47389-409-9

CIP data records for this title are available from the British Library

Pen & Sword Books Limited incorporates the imprints of Atlas, Archaeology, Aviation, Discovery, Family History, Fiction, History, Maritime, Military, Military Classics, Politics, Select, Transport, True Crime, Air World, Frontline Publishing, Leo Cooper, Remember When, Seaforth Publishing, The Praetorian Press, Wharncliffe Local History, Wharncliffe Transport, Wharncliffe True Crime and White Owl.

For more information on our books, please visit
www.pen-and-sword.co.uk, email enquiries@pen-and-sword.co.uk
or write to us at the above address.

Printed and bound by TJ International Ltd. PL28 8RW

Typeset in 10/13pt Palatino

CONTENTS

PROLOGUE

AT 13.15 HOURS Greenwich Mean Time on September 13th, 1940, the Empire flying-boat Clare, Captain J.T. Kirton, of British Overseas Airways Corporation, took off from the waters of Poole harbour in Dorset and set course westwards towards the Atlantic.

She trailed behind her, across the smooth harbour waters facing the haphazard little huddle of buildings on the quay, a widening wake of troubled white foam. She left behind her a still more troubled sky. The weightiest formations of the Luftwaffe were ranging over southern England, thrusting at the people of London in the longest daylight raids they had yet endured.

By mid-afternoon Clare had alighted on the waters of the Shannon at Foynes, in Eire, where there was no war save in the anxious minds of the people. The captain had hoped to continue his flight that evening, but when he consulted the meteorological information he was compelled to postpone his departure.

All next day the flying-boat lay on the Shannon, her crew turning to the radio for news of the mounting Battle of Britain. While they waited, another Empire flying-boat arrived from Poole, bringing with her a bundle of London newspapers which was stowed aboard Clare. The following day, September 15th, the tighter squadrons of the Royal Air Force were compelling the Luftwaffe to the tremendous climax of their daylight assault; 185 German aircraft were to be shot down before sunset. Before all that total had been reached, Clare had left her moorings on the Shannon, and at 18.10 hours G.M.T. she took off for Newfoundland. When the 185th German aircraft fell from the sky, Clare was already moving steadily through the mists and cloud over the Atlantic, flying on the Great Circle route to Newfoundland.

The two pilots, Captain Kirton and Captain J.S. Shakespeare, and the navigator, Captain T.H. Farnsworth, kept watch on the flight-deck throughout the night, navigating by the stars when they could see them through the clouds and by dead reckoning when they could not. Of the ocean beneath them they could see nothing, frequently nothing of the sky above; their world was contained for that night in the warmly lit flight-deck of the flying-boat, their thoughts on the mechanics of flight and the continual problem of navigation. Though even those necessities, one of them said, could not shut out altogether from their minds troubled speculation on the outcome of the air war which lay behind them, or remembrances of the growing number of their friends who had gone into the R.A.F. and who were losing their lives.

Their own immediate task, of course, predominated. Through the windows they could see nothing but a drift of darkness in which hung the firm, steady outline of the wing structure upon which they sometimes shone a feeble torchlight, seeking traces of ice formation by which, as it happened, they were not troubled. In the young daylight of September 16th, they sighted the Newfoundland coast with its hinterland of desolation sprinkled with many rivers and lakes.

Soon after they had crossed the coast they received a radio message to say that Botwood, their destination, was covered in thick local fog, with the cloud base at only 150 feet and visibility of less than 200 yards. Here was anxiety. Botwood lies on the shores of the saltwater Bay of Exploits, behind which rise hills to a height of several hundred feet; the amount of petrol remaining in the tanks after an Atlantic crossing did not encourage delay.

At 11.40 hours G.M.T., circling over Botwood, the crew saw that the only piece of cloud in the whole sky lay directly over Botwood itself and their alighting area. They circled for 20 minutes, cautiously descending. At last a gap appeared in the cloud, and through this gap they alighted on the Bay of Exploits.

They remained there for little more than an hour before taking off again for the United States. There was another brief halt at Boucherville near Montreal; then at dusk they were circling at a height of 1,000 feet, less than that of the topmost buildings, round the sky-line of New York. No matter how troubled the world, nobody can contemplate, after an Atlantic flight, anything other than the fascination of New York from the air. These merchant airmen commented to each other, as they always did on such an occasion, on this remarkable instance of the way in which nature anticipates man. They had all flown for years on the great Empire air-routes and were well acquainted with that most curious and massive rock-formation on the Baluchistan coast, just east of Jiwani, which thrusts up pinnacles in a striking imitation of the New York skyline.

On this occasion, the metropolitan spectacle was more beautiful than usual. As Clare made a circuit over the East River, as far as Queensborough Bridge, the lights of New York were just beginning to glitter through the dusk. "We could see the dark pinnacles of skyscrapers in which batches of light would suddenly twinkle, one after the other," one of the captains described it. "The lights twinkled and spread all over the city, until the whole thing reminded me strongly of a heaving mass of molten brass in a foundry. Have you ever seen it? A great city lighting up at dusk is just like that; for molten brass, just as it starts to cool, twinkles all over with lights.

"But when we had alighted at La Guardia airport, moored up and gone ashore, we were all, I think, a little silent. It was impossible to escape the contrast between the two ends of our Atlantic flight. We had left behind the pitch-black cities of Britain, lit only by searchlights, bomb-flashes and fires, but full of people confident of victory; we had arrived at a city sparkling with light, where, as it seemed to us, the number of people who had any hopes in Britain's survival, though increasing, was still very small. We met the warmest admiration for Britain's stubbornness, but little feeling that it was any more than stubbornness, or that the fight would not soon be ended. Though the news of the great air victory of September 15th, so amazing that many could scarcely believe it, was flooding the city with a faint, new hope."

This very Atlantic flight by Clare did more to nurture and foster that new hope in America than probably any other single factor. There was, firstly, the fact that she had been able to make the flight at all. It seemed unbelievable that an unarmed flying-boat could have taken off from the midst of the Battle of Britain and flown calmly to New York, just as in peacetime; yet there she lay at her moorings at La Guardia, her camouflaged wings and hull the only sign of war. It was assumed that she had left Britain under a strong fighter escort; but there had been no escort – the fighters were engaged in more pressing duties – only an unarmed merchantman, flying alone.

Then there was that bundle of London newspapers which she had carried to New York. German propaganda, powerful in America at that time, was boasting loudly that London was being reduced to a vacant shell, that Fleet Street had been bombed out of action. Here, in these newspapers speedily distributed to the newspaper offices of America, was visual proof to the contrary. The American papers seized upon it with delight. Many of them made photostatic copies of the front pages of these London newspapers, and spread them across their own front pages.

Typical was the *New York Post* of September 18th. It led its front page with a banner headline, "EXTRA EXTRA. LONDON NEWSPAPERS IN BUSINESS AS USUAL." Below that it published a photostat of a London newspaper, telling the story of the longest day raid and the bombing of Buckingham Palace, with a photograph of a Hurricane swooping in triumph over a fallen foe. "Bombs are dropping in or near Fleet-street every night," read the New York Post's leading story, "and the plants of two great London newspapers have already been damaged, but all are continuing to publish more or less as usual. This copy reached New York yesterday aboard the flying-boat Clare, only three days after it had rolled off the presses around the corner from Fleet Street. It was edited and printed under the heaviest German air bombardment of the war to date, but its columns do not emphasise that. In fact, the traditional British understatement is applied to the account of the raid then in progress ... It will be seen from the front-page headlines that there is no attempt to conceal bad news, such as the bombing of Buckingham Palace." The writer then analysed in detail the news of this London newspaper, and added good-humoured, admiring comment on the decorum and normality of the advertisements.

Similar headlines appeared throughout the United States. America's front page, for which Dr. Goebbels was then striving with all his resources, was captured for Britain on that crucial day by the small packet of London newspapers which a British aircraft had flown across the Atlantic. Englishmen who were there at the time noted with delight the vivid impression that was made on the American people, the sudden lifting of foreboding.

This story of Clare's flight to New York during the blitz on Britain is but one incident in the long and honourable story of the British merchant air service during the war, though it illustrates more neatly than most the value of our airmen who have flown unarmed through the war skies, taking risks in the common cause as readily as their brothers in the Royal Air Force. Security reasons have prevented much being said hitherto of the work of these airmen, as worthy and gallant, in its own element, as that of the merchant seamen on theirs.

In this book is told for the first time something of their war history, something of their lives and their achievements in linking up the battlefronts – at times cut off from any direct land or sea contacts with Britain – and in transporting supplies through the new, dangerous and often uncharted regions of the air.

PART I

THE SKIES OF EUROPE

By 1929, Imperial Airways Ltd. had pushed its regular weekly service from Great Britain to India. The leisurely four-engine biplane *Hanno* was typical of the land-based passenger aircraft of those days. (US Library of Congress)

CHAPTER 1

Nineteen Million Miles a Year

THE YEAR 1944 WAS the 25th anniversary of British commercial aviation. On the morning of August 25th, 1919, three aircraft left London for Paris with paying passengers.

Most Englishmen would be hard put to it to give much of an account of how the merchant air service has grown since then; before the war, Britain did not rank high among air-minded nations, doubtless because of the geography and climate of these small islands. In the future, nothing less will do than a strong public realisation of the urgent necessity of our air lines. In no matter how co-operative a spirit the air routes of the world are then flown, there will still be keen competition. The United States' aviation went on to fly over the world. The sturdy Dutchmen had created, in KLM, an external air line of high efficiency. The Russians, we learn, had a strong internal aviation before the war and henceforth may well intend to look towards foreign skies for trade. The shortest link between the countries of the Commonwealth will lie in the sky.

Throughout those 25 years a comparatively small number of people in Britain appreciated the urgencies of air commerce. Apart from the smaller internal air lines which grew up, there were two big companies dealing with overseas routes, Imperial Airways Ltd., concentrating mostly on the longer flights, and British Airways Ltd. concentrating on European routes. Imperial Airways had a big associate company in Australia, Qantas Empire Airways. The air crews in Britain were as well acquainted with the intricacies of European flying as any group of airmen in the world. Those of Imperial Airways, a stalwart band of captains, had done more air pioneering of distant lands than any other collection of men could claim.

In 1927 they plied regularly over the desert between Cairo and Basra. By 1929 they had pushed their regular weekly air service from England to India, by 1933 to Burma, and by 1934, in co-operation with Qantas Empire Airways, onwards to Australia; two years later they included Hong Kong and, in 1940, New Zealand. In 1931 they connected London by a regular service to Tanganyika, and in the following year to Cape Town. After earlier survey flights by the Royal Air Force, the captains were making frequent flights in the early 1930's over the vast jungles of Central Africa, where the greenery closes over the gap torn in the trees after only a few hours if by mischance an aircraft should crash; in 1936 they had pioneered a regular service between Cairo and West Africa.

In the three years immediately before the war the great Empire trunk routes were fully established. In 1937 began the experimental series of flying-boat flights between Southampton and New York; by 1939 they had increased to eight round trips, carrying mail, in late summer.

It would be as well to complete here the picture of British air routes just before the war. In addition to the Empire and Atlantic routes, Imperial Airways were flying regular services in Europe to Paris, Le Touquet, Brussels, Cologne, Frankfort, Basle and Zurich. British Airways linked London with Paris, Berlin, Warsaw, Brussels, Frankfort, Budapest, Hamburg, Copenhagen and Stockholm, with a night mail service to Cologne, Hanover and Berlin.

More than a dozen smaller companies flew between big centres in Britain and to neighbouring islands. Some of these companies crossed also, in season, to holiday resorts on the Continental coast.

To round off the picture there were the 81 light aeroplane clubs (in Britain and Northern Ireland), most of them receiving Government subsidy, together with a number of gliding clubs.

In 1934 the most ambitious air mail scheme ever conceived was proposed for speeding communications within the Empire. It was known as the Empire air mail scheme, or the "all-up"' mail scheme; briefly, it was proposed to carry all mail between this country and the Empire by air, without any surcharge. Thus the cost of sending a letter from London to Australia was the same as from London to Brighton – 1½d. A completely new fleet of flying-boats was ordered to accommodate this freight, together with passengers. They were the Short C-class Empire flying-boats, the first of which was delivered in 1937, the remaining 31 following quickly. These flying-boats became the basic fleet of Imperial Airways, and the "all-up" air mail scheme was completed and in full operation by 1938. It may be said at once that that fleet of flying-boats, diminished by enemy action, was still, after the fifth year of war, flying efficiently on the Empire routes.

After the report of the Cadman Committee came a fundamental change in the structure of British external aviation. Hitherto it had been operated by commercial companies drawing financial assistance from the Government. In November 1938 the Secretary of State for Air announced in the House of Commons that the two companies, Imperial Airways and British Airways, were to be merged into a single Corporation, to be the single "chosen instrument" of the United Kingdom Government in skies outside the British Isles.

From June 1939 the two companies, though nominally still in existence, were working together as a single Corporation. The British Overseas

Two of Imperial Airways' aircraft at Ruthba in the 1930s. Taking off in the background is *Hanno*, **whilst in the foreground is** *Apollo*. (US Library of Congress)

Airways Act passed through Parliament and became law in August 1939. In November the British Overseas Airways Corporation was established with Sir John (later Lord) Reith as chairman, but the undertakings of the two companies were not formally handed over until April 1st, 1940. On that day the Corporation issued £4¼ millions of 3 per cent. Airways Stock, guaranteed as to capital and interest by the Treasury, but carrying no voting rights. The Act envisaged that the stock would eventually be issued to the public, but owing to war conditions the stock was subscribed by the National Debt Commissioners and will be held by them until a public offer is made. From the sums thus received, the Corporation paid about £3¼ millions to the two air line companies in respect of the undertakings which they handed over.

At the outbreak of war the two companies, by virtue of their agreements with the Secretary of State for Air, placed the whole of their undertakings at his disposal. This arrangement was continued when the Corporation took over. While management is left to the Board of the Corporation, policy matters such as decisions on the routes and frequencies to be operated and the traffic to be carried are controlled by the Secretary of State, who meets from public funds the deficiency on each year's working. Thus for the whole of the war British overseas air services have worked, without thought of profit, for the good of the national war effort.

Indeed, during the course of the war quite a large number of Royal Air Force men have been seconded to the merchant service.

When war began, the fleet which passed under the control of the Air Minister consisted of 82 aircraft. There were 17 Short S.23 Empire flying-boats which have been described, and 5 similar Short S.30 flying-boats. There was the famous Mayo composite flying-boat and seaplane, and one other seaplane. The other main components of the fleet were 5 "A" class Atalanta

A.W. 15 land-planes, 7 "H" class H.P. 42 land-planes, 9 "D" class D.H. 86B land-planes, 5 Lockheed 10A land-planes, 7 Lockheed 14 land-planes, 12 "E" class Ensign land-planes, and 5 "F" class D.H. 91 Frobisher land-planes.

The men (and women who were later recruited) who flew these aircraft or tended them on the ground, were scattered throughout all those parts of the world which the routes traversed, and their jobs, though differently organised, were similar to those of the ground staffs of the Royal Air Force.

Many of them have not seen Britain since the war began, nor are they likely to do so until some time after its end. They live in the burning heat of deserts, in jungles alongside the upper reaches of great rivers, in malarial swamps, on distant islands in lonely seas. The women employees, many of whom came into the service during the war, are not posted to the remoter stations. But they are scattered over the rest of the routes, working along-side the men, often in tropical conditions; working, too, at the benches and machines in the engineering shops.

The air crews are the men who keep open, day in and day out, some 54,000 miles of air routes over many parts of the world, ranging from the Arctic to South Africa, from the Atlantic coast of America to the eastern coast of India – routes that are carried on by their Australian and New Zealand counterparts and by the air lines of Canada, South Africa and India. Over these routes they fly just short of 19,000,000 miles a year. There can rarely have been a moment, throughout the war, when aircraft of the British merchant air service have not been flying somewhere along the routes.

The captains do not conform to the traditional type of airmen which has been impressed on the public mind by the great exploits of the Royal Air Force – young, reckless in gallantry. These captains have a different sort of task to carry out, more closely resembling that of a merchant captain at sea. Theirs is to get their passengers and cargo safely to their destination, no matter through what circumstances of weather, in the most economical fashion and with the greatest possible punctuality.

It is a task that has been immeasurably hampered by war conditions, when radio and meteorological aids to navigation have been either much reduced or altogether lacking. On occasion, only men of the long flying experience of these captains could have succeeded, or would have made the attempt. For their experience is unchallenged anywhere in the world. Many of them have been flying continuously for between 25 and 30 years. There are as many captains in the service of British Overseas Airways who have flown more than a million miles each, as in all the rest of the world put together.

It will be seen, then, that many of the captains who fly under the Civil Air Ensign – a light blue ensign with a dark blue cross edged with white, the Union Jack in the corner – and who fly the house flag of British Overseas

Airways, with its golden speedbird insignia worked on an imperial blue burgee, are men advanced into their middle years. There are some of 45 years of age and more who still fly the regular routes. Some wear ribbons of decorations which they gained in the war of 1914, and they flew often through the battle zones of this last one.

They have proved, as this book will show, that they rival the younger pilots in courage and endurance. They have flown always unarmed, often into skies crowded with battle. Some of them have been lost to enemy fighters, some to the increased risks in wartime of long-distance flying. For two wartime winters they were the only men in the world who maintained a regular two-way service through the formidable skies of the North Atlantic.

"The Secretary of State to-day paid tribute to the Royal Air Force personnel," said Captain Harold Balfour in Parliament, "and I think it is appropriate that the House should also pay tribute to the captains and crews who are running daily on the civil routes. They are operating week in and week out, regardless of weather, driving their aircraft along these routes, facing not only the very frequent hazards, but the inevitable risk of enemy interference. I can tell the House that there has been a toll among the personnel, from enemy action. They have died in the country's service."

The Short S.17 Kent flying boat *Satyrus* pictured on Sea of Galilee, circa 1935. *Satyrus* remained in service until 1938. (US Library of Congress)

The Short S.30 Empire-class flying boat *Clio* **taking off or landing at Palestine circa 1939.** (US Library of Congress)

CHAPTER 2

Stand by for War

ON A LOVELY South African spring day the Empire flying-boat Clio had taken off from the land-locked harbour at Durban and was flying northwards along the coast, bound for Southampton. She had refuelled at Beira and was making for Mozambique in the bright sunshine, the water below deep blue, a white line of foam on the yellow beach, and patches of bright green gleaming above submerged islands and rocks close to the surface.

The 18 passengers were snoozing in their comfortable chairs in the cabins. Some white cloud drifted towards the horizon. Southbound, the captain had seen the German liner Watussi drop anchor well inside the neutral anchorage at Mozambique. But his thoughts were on the peace of the day rather than such matters, when the radio officer stood up abruptly from his seat and hurried forward with a scribbled message, "England has declared war on Germany." The captain glanced at it, and automatically sent the news down to the passengers. Then they continued their peaceful flight to Southampton docks, and reached London on the usual "Ocean Liner Pullman Special."

A short time before this radio message reached Clio off the coast of Portuguese East Africa, another merchant air crew was driving down to the quay at Southampton, where the flying-boat Cabot lay at her moorings. They had been scheduled to take off the previous day, but the flight had been postponed for 24 hours without any reason given. The airmen sat in the car by the quay, listening to its radio, over which they heard Mr. Chamberlain announce the declaration of war. Then they moved quietly out to Cabot and took off for the United States.

During the early hours of the following morning, while they were flying through low cloud against a strong headwind, their radio picked up an SOS message from the stricken S.S. Athenia on the ocean somewhere beneath them. They arrived at a New York of staring headlines, delivered a present of grouse which they had carried for President Roosevelt, and, weary as they were, had to submit to enthusiastic fêting by the Americans.

It was in such a manner that merchant airmen scattered all over the world routes learned of the outbreak of war. At home in England the actual declaration had been anticipated by a week. Stand-by messages were signalled to headquarters throughout the world. The following day, while the flying-boats were being diverted to the western side of France, and while ground staff were already being withdrawn from distant stations in Europe, Horatius took off with the first RAF war load, and delivered it to Paris. On August 30th Fortune left for Karachi with 11 senior Army officers, avoiding Italian territory on the way.

At Croydon airport, traditional gateway to London, there was a marked contrast. All equipment had been quietly packed up, and a goods train was standing ready at Norwood Junction to carry it to the West Country. But outwardly the airport seemed as busy as usual, save that the night service to Paris had been cancelled as the French had forbidden all night-flying over their country. On August 31st came official instructions. Continental services were to stop; only the Empire services would continue as usual. Croydon was to be evacuated.

Within 24 hours the airport was empty of all activity, and British Overseas Airways had transferred itself to Bristol. Only three aircraft remained at desolate Croydon, all unserviceable. The Ensigns and F-class air liners had flown to Coventry, whence they were scattered to different RAF airfields, waiting to transport men and equipment to their war stations in France. Camouflaged overnight, they were soon hard at it. Captain H.H. Perry, one of the oldest of the merchant captains, who had flown his Ensign to the airfield of a Fairey Battle squadron, took the first load. He packed his aircraft full of RAF ground engineers and equipment, and was given sealed orders to be opened in flight. He put his first load down in a big field near Rheims, a party of bewildered men who gazed around the empty countryside in dismay.

"Where are the hangars?" they asked, "Where is the Mess?" Perry laughed, and told them that they had a nice big cosy field all to themselves, and somebody would be along to see them in the afternoon. On the way back he met the Battle squadron itself flying out, and later in the day he returned with a second party. All the other air liners, then and subsequently, were engaged on the same task – ferrying the ground crews, equipment and stores of the RAF to their French stations. The captains all commented on the smoothness of the organisation. Much of the credit for that goes to an organisation called National Air Communications, a convenient title for the co-ordination of all civil aviation activities for the furtherance of the war effort.

This body was necessary because the Air Navigation Restriction Order which came into force with the outbreak of war prohibited any civil flying over the United Kingdom without special permit. All unnecessary flying stopped abruptly, but all other useful air services were grouped together under National Air Communications, and their effort was directed to a common plan. As far as was possible the aircraft were left to the management of their own companies and their own crews. Eighteen internal air line companies placed their fleets, personnel and organisation at the service of the Air Ministry, and were gathered into the collective air-transport scheme. A number of the pre-war internal services, particularly those running to islands off the coast, were soon set into operation again, but the remainder of available air transport was turned to the task of getting our men and supplies across to France.

The great overseas routes were left almost unchanged, except that, to conserve effort, Empire air mail was carried only on the payment of a surcharge. The home airport for the flying-boats was transferred from Southampton to Poole harbour. The marine gear was sent round by sea in the flying-boat launches, one of which broke down with engine failure just off the Needles. Heavy seas were running in a strong south-easterly gale, in spite of which the accompanying launch took her in tow, and brought her over the bar into Poole harbour on a day when the local coastguards had been unable to put to sea.

A number of special flights were commenced on military request. Secret documents, and then some secret radio equipment, were flown from Britain to Malta. Some British Army technicians with special radio equipment were flown from Egypt to Greece, whence they made their way northwards to the rear of the Polish battlefront. The value of merchant airmen in wartime was thus quickly proved.

The series of mail flights by the flying-boats Cabot and Caribou across the Atlantic was continued in spite of the war until the end of September, when it was intended to finish in any case.

The Clipper flying-boats of Pan-American Airways, the counterpart in the United States of our own Imperial Airways, had by that time commenced a passenger service across the Atlantic, carrying Americans of eminence, mostly bound for this country. The Pan-American service ended, owing to the Neutrality Act, at Foynes, so our own flying-boats ran a shuttle from Foynes to Poole to meet the Clippers whenever they arrived.

All our European air services had stopped at once on the declaration of war, with the exception of a weekly service from Scotland to Norway, Sweden and Finland which had been opened only in the last week of August. One other service, that to Paris, was soon resumed.

There was another type of service which merchant airmen rendered to those early days of war, and which they have continued to render ever since. Some time before the war the Department of Civil Aviation at the Air Ministry had contemplated the possibility of much worse conditions on the outbreak of war than actually occurred. It was thought that enemy bombing might become so intense that road and rail communications might break down inside Britain. A number of pilots above any likely military age were therefore recruited to run emergency communications flights; it was thought that they could also be useful in ferrying aircraft about the country. They were enrolled and administered by Mr. G. d'Erlanger, subsequently a director of British Overseas Airways. Soon after war broke out there were 20 of them, known as the Air Transport Auxiliary – "Ancient and Tattered Airmen" – as they dubbed themselves.

As communications did not break down under enemy bombing a few of them were put to the task of ferrying new aircraft to the RAF squadrons. At the height of the battle which was soon to follow they were flying new aircraft to France itself. Afterwards they grew, in this country, into an organisation several hundreds strong, flying Service aircraft in their thousands from the factories straight to the squadrons, and thus relieving the RAF of much anxiety and manpower. But the story of their wartime achievements is too considerable to be told in detail here, and deserves a separate account.

So, throughout the first few quiet months of the war, Britain's merchant air service continued in somewhat routine fashion over most of its old routes and a few new. The most important new route was that from Britain to Portugal. It was delayed at first until Spain gave us permission to fly over her territory, but by the summer of 1940 a regular service had been started to Lisbon. With a few minor interruptions, it has continued ever since, and has proved one of the most valuable links between Britain and the outside world throughout the war. Much of its burden was soon undertaken by Dutchmen of KLM, operating under charter to British Overseas Airways, and maintaining with very few aircraft a performance which it would be hard to beat for regularity.

At the Lisbon end, crews mixed into that curious atmosphere that pervades any neutral junction; it is, after all, strange to place one's baggage on a customs counter opposite to a German traveller submitting his, to draw up an aircraft on the airfield side by side with those of the Lufthansa, to encounter the then inimical Italian airmen in the lounge of an hotel. There was also the grim side of the situation typified by a particularly cruel attack, much later in the war, by German fighters on one of the KLM aircraft which was carrying women and children from Lisbon; the incident was widely reported, since among the passengers, all of whom lost their lives, was Mr. Leslie Howard the actor.

Chief enemy in that winter of 1939-40 was not the Hun, but the perennial enemy of flying, the weather. In mid-January snow, frost and ice spread all over Europe, and from station after station messages accumulated reporting that flying was impossible. The Norwegian service was the first to be cancelled, on reports that snowdrifts were piled on Stavanger airfield.

The luxurious interior of an Imperial Airways Empire-class flying boat, almost certainly *Clio*, **pictured before the war.** (US Library of Congress)

Poole harbour was frosting with ice, a strong mistral was blowing at Marseilles. The flying-boats on the Empire routes, lying frozen at their moorings, became 3, 5, 9, as much as 13 days late. The waters at Marseilles were icing over, throughout southern England the airfields were buried under snow. Weather at Bordeaux was so bad that one Hudson had to overfly the place, and make an emergency landing on the beach at Jersey. At St. Nazaire there were dangerous ice floes at low tide, and only one mooring buoy remained free for the flying-boats. Early in February there was so rapid a thaw in England that the airfields were under water. Just as these troubles were fading away in the early spring, trouble of another kind broke out on the Persian Gulf.

Two rival sheikhs, at Dubai, where there is a flying-boat stop, and nearby Sharjah, where the airfield lies close by the old fort, decided to have a local war. The British Overseas Airways station manager persuaded them to confine hostilities to the hours of darkness, so that passengers could be driven about in the daytime and refuelling stops could still be made, but night-stopping of aircraft was inadvisable. That meant a re-arrangement of the Empire route timetable. Just when that had been fixed up, the airfield on the island of Bahrain, the next stop, chose to flood itself during exceptional winds and tide.

But these were only the normal trials of airways; they had nothing to do with the war. The impact of that was not to be long delayed. On April 9th the German invasion poured into Norway.

Two of the most famous flying-boats of the merchant fleet, Cabot and Caribou, transferred to the Royal Air Force, were speedily involved. As they flew into battle with their normal air crews, temporarily released for service with the Air Force, their story properly forms part of this record.

Cabot and Caribou were the two flying-boats which had flown the transatlantic mail service in the summer of 1939, completing the schedule after war had broken out. From the start, they had been earmarked for long-range reconnaissance. As the war proceeded quietly it was thought that they might still be available for the merchant routes. It was then proposed that they should be put back on the Atlantic run in the summer of 1940, possibly inaugurating the first British passenger service to America. But the RAF needed them.

With Captain Gordon Store in command of Cabot, and Captain S.G. Long of Caribou, the two flying-boats patrolled for a time as part of the RAF Coastal Command. During the Norwegian invasion they were assigned to the task of taking an RAF unit to set up radiolocation stations in that country. Cabot took off with the first load, and alighted on Saturday, May 4th, at Harstad, the main Allied base for operations against Narvik – a little port busy that day with warships and transports, bustling wharves, troops moving ashore. The town had been considerably bombed, and there were air raids while Cabot lay in the harbour, but in the main streets of the town girls still walked about in ski-clothes, and children ran on miniature skis down the slopes.

The whole party slept on board that night, taking off next day for the small port of Bodo, some 10 miles south of Narvik. They ran out the Norwegian flag from sheer habit when they alighted – commercial aircraft always fly the national flag of whichever country they are visiting.

Here was another idyllic little scene – the compact buildings of the town, the snow mountains behind, even the church bells ringing merrily on this bright Sunday morning. A small boat put out from shore towards them, carrying a policeman to inform them that the church bells were not so merry after all; that was the air raid alert. The raid passed without mishap, and the party set to work to unload equipment from Cabot into dinghies. As they were doing so, Caribou came in from Scotland, alighting on the water nearby.

The two captains went ashore for a conference, and had just learned that the harbour possessed no anti-aircraft defences when the bells pealed again. A Heinkel float-plane had evidently seen the flying-boats and was diving in a long spiral towards them. The captains dashed for the dinghies, and Captain Store managed to get aboard Cabot, slip her moorings, and start her taxying before the Heinkel came in low for its first attack. His crew had jumped to their guns, one of them abandoning some steaks he was frying in the galley, in the absence of the air-gunner cook who had rowed over to Caribou to borrow some gravy salt. Captain Store was wounded in the foot and several of his crew had narrow escapes in the eight machine-gun attacks made by the Heinkel. The wing-roots of Cabot were smoking and she was holed in many places, so the captain ran her gently on to the mud at one end of the harbour. Captain Store hopped out on one leg, hugging a machine-gun.

Caribou had suffered more severely. In the last German attack four of her crew, one of them an RAF gunner, had been wounded, she was badly damaged, and her bilges reeked of escaping fuel. She was also run aground lest she might sink. The wounded were put into hospital in the town, while the others set to work to clear all the equipment from the two flying-boats. They had emptied Cabot and were working on Caribou when another Heinkel attacked, setting Caribou on fire with a bomb and burning her out completely.

Cabot floated on the tide that night – it was continual daylight – and she was towed up the coast by two motor-boats and hidden between a high cliff and a large rock. German aircraft searched up and down the coast for her next day, finding her at last and firing her with incendiary bullets. She also was a total loss. The crews were taken back to Britain in a destroyer.

The loss of two flying-boats was no great matter in a campaign in which Norway was lost. But the loss of those two particular long-range flying-boats meant at least the postponement of hopes of a British transatlantic service that year.

CHAPTER 3

Hubbub at Bordeaux

THE FIRST SHOCK of the German invasion of Holland and Belgium had small effect on our overseas air routes. The services to Paris and on the Empire route left later the same day. So abrupt was the invasion that the KLM (Dutch) and SABENA (Belgian) air lines, which had resumed their services to England from Amsterdam and Brussels soon after the war started, had been operating on the previous day. Eight of the Belgian aircraft flew across to this country, and several of the Dutch arrived in the following few days.

Almost the whole of our own merchant air service, other than those aircraft on the Empire routes, was concentrated at once to rush supplies to our Forces in France. Captains and air crews toiled ceaselessly, some of them making several flights a day. They flew completely unarmed and without armour. For the first time they were flying into war-infested skies, and several of them had narrow escapes from enemy fighters over Northern France.

The cargoes that they carried were varied, but the bulk of them was food and ammunition for our forward troops. They plied back and forth day and night, as calmly as though they were on normal service. After a night delivery-flight, some of the crews arrived back in England, changed their clothes, took a bath perhaps, and set off again on a day delivery to France.

On the night of May 22nd-23rd, for example, Captain G.R. Buxton took an Ensign to Merville, to bring food to some of our troops who were temporarily isolated in that neighbourhood. He unloaded, returned to England, being shot up by a trawler in the Channel on the way, and immediately joined a small formation which was starting with another cargo of food and ammunition for the same destination. Under a Hurricane escort they arrived without incident, landing in a big field, the crews stripping to the shirt and starting to unload the supplies themselves.

At that moment a crowd of Messerschmitts appeared overhead. The Hurricanes engaged them in a long dogfight, watched with interest by the airmen on the ground, since it was the first that most of them had seen in this war. "It lasted for about 20 minutes," said one captain, "with aircraft coming down, people baling out and everything; most exciting." By that time the Hurricanes were running out of fuel and had to fly away. The merchant airmen continued to dump the supplies from their aircraft.

Suddenly two more Messerschmitts came in low out of the sun in a machine-gun attack. Without even a revolver with which to reply, the airmen ducked for whatever shelter there was, and watched one of the aircraft, the Ensign Elysean, strafed from wingtip to wingtip while the radio officer lay crouched beneath its tail; it caught fire and burnt out. Most of the other aircraft were holed and somewhat damaged, but they could all still fly. The crews dashed into them.

Captain J.M.H. Hoare and First Officer Tettenborn, whose Ensign had been destroyed, climbed into a D.H.86. Their radio officer jumped aboard an Ensign which was taking off with its door open. On the return flight across France the aircraft flew through intense anti-aircraft fire. Two of them were shot down near Calais. The crews were taken prisoner; Captain Hoare was killed. Captain S.T.B. Cripps (an RAF pilot of the last war) had his Ensign badly shot-up over Calais. He came across the Channel on three engines. Another cut out over Folkestone and he landed safely at Lympne on two engines and one wheel. The rest of the aircraft (more or less damaged) reached their home base safely. As an indication of the intensity at which these airmen were working at that time, Captain Allan Andrew, who had piloted another of the Ensigns to Merville, took off again that same afternoon for Rouen, carrying fully charged aircraft batteries to the fighter squadrons who were engaged in such heavy combat that they had run their batteries down and could not get them recharged in time. The only enemy action he encountered at Rouen was "a little bombing."

The service to Paris, of vital importance at this time, was kept running as long as possible. On June 1st Captain G.R. Buxton piloted the Ensign Ettrick to Le Bourget. He and his crew were lunching in the restaurant when they were bombed "good and hard." Some 300 bombs were dropped on the airport and its neighbourhood, 200 people being killed in the little village of Le Blanc-Mesnil over the way, and an unknown number more on the airfield itself, on which most of the buildings were partially destroyed. The passengers, who had been waiting by the luggage which was just about to be loaded into Ettrick, were hurried into a shelter, the last man down, a French porter, being killed as he ran. Captain Buxton had gone into the cellar of the restaurant, but found it "a bit fierce'" down there, as the building received a direct hit, a water-main burst, and smoke was being sucked down from the fires above. He came up, almost walked into a falling bomb, and was wounded in the thigh. The Ensign was considerably damaged, although the captain at once climbed into her, tried her controls, and thought he could take off; the French authorities, however, would not permit, as the airfield was plastered with time bombs. Eventually Ettrick had to be abandoned where she stood.

It was clear that Le Bourget could no longer be used. The terminus was shifted farther and farther south, first to Guyancourt, then to Tours. One of the captains who carried out a few flights to that airfield has only one notable memory of it – of Mr. Winston Churchill and M. Reynaud pacing back and forth in conversation, the Prime Minister in an old grey coat and grey felt hat, "looking terribly haggard and worried."

The whole of this part of the story stands out against the background of the German advance across France – the rumble of tanks, panicky rumours flashing round airfields that the leading Huns were only a few miles distant, confusion, desperation. The urgent task was to bring home to Britain as many key-men as possible, and for this the merchant air fleet, small as it was, was most suitable. It concentrated, for the most part, on bringing back air crews and technicians of the RAF.

Every serviceable aircraft was organised under National Air Communications for the task; each flew back and forth between France and Britain to the limit of its powers. The airmen flew over roads crowded with refugees, over villages and cities smoking with bombardment, sometimes into the thick of combats between our own fighters and the German bombers. They landed on airfields that were on the verge of panic, struggled to obtain enough fuel for the return journey, and came home crowded from nose to tail with their rescued.

They made some strange flights. Captain Cripps flew an Ensign to pick up a party from Nantes, only to find the airfield completely deserted, with aircraft burning all over its surface. His second captain jumped out of the aircraft to salvage an abandoned bicycle. Not wishing to return empty, they made for Jersey, and took a hand in the air evacuation from that island which was being staunchly organised by Jersey Airways Ltd. They filled the Ensign with evacuees and brought them over to Exeter.

On June 17th, a small merchant air fleet was organised to help evacuate an RAF squadron from an airfield near Lyons. They intended to refuel their aircraft at Bordeaux and Marseilles on the way – by this time Bordeaux had become the most northerly French airfield which they could use. Captain Perry was the first to arrive at Bordeaux. "I spent some time taxying back and forth across the airfield, trying to get some petrol out of somebody," he related, "getting none, and damaging my tail wheel in the process. Suddenly a French officer whom I knew came out of one of the hangars and told me, with a white face, that France had given in. By this time the airfield was an extraordinary sight. Some other Ensigns and some D.H.86s of my party were coming in from the north, all seeking petrol. An RAF Bombay came in from the south. I gave it up for a few minutes and slipped into a shack to get a cup of coffee. Inside I met my son who, unbeknown to me, was flying one of the other aircraft in our fleet." (Captain Perry's son was later reported missing from a RAF operational flight.) "I asked him what he was doing, and he said, 'Same as you, Dad.'

"Then I started to look for petrol in earnest. I taxied over to a dump, seized a bowser, and managed to get the Ensign filled before the angry French bowser-crew found out. It seemed hopeless to try to push on to Lyons, so I went across to ask the RAF crew of the Bombay how things stood. They turned out to be part of the squadron we had been sent to help; they said they were the last aircraft out, and the Huns were already in the place. Some of the other captains decided to try to push on nevertheless, but they had to put back from Marseilles, and most of the aircraft were later destroyed by the Germans at Bordeaux.

"By this time a lot of French aircraft were coming in. They came from all sorts of directions, putting down where they could, and the crashes were mounting rapidly. I decided to make for home, managed to get off in spite of my broken tailwheel, and got home without incident, except that some Hurricanes edged me away from St. Nazaire, where they were dealing with Huns bombing the place."

One of the Ensigns which arrived to refuel at Bordeaux on that same confused morning was piloted by Captain L.V. Messenger. He had just flown Sir Samuel Hoare to Madrid, to assume his ambassadorial post, and was on his way back to Britain. He had been refused permission to spend the night at Madrid, so had stopped at Lisbon instead, taking off in the morning with the normal load of passengers, and without any knowledge of the impending French capitulation. He arrived at Bordeaux in the middle of the tumult, learned the news with dismay, managed somehow to get some petrol, filled up every corner of his aircraft with RAF men, and took off at once.

As he taxied across the airfield a car ran out after him, so he quickly swung round and took off right over it. "I thought the man in the car was trying to stop me," he said, "but I found out later he was only wanting to warn me to avoid Nantes on the way home, because the Huns were bombing it. We found that out when we got there – it was getting a hell of a pasting. I pulled quickly into cloud, and we flew on – there was nothing else to do. We had not had any lunch, but we had on board some particularly fine lobsters which we had bought in Lisbon. Reflecting that, if we were to be shot down, it might as well be with full stomachs, we pulled out the lobsters and had an excellent meal over Nantes, to the accompaniment of the bombing below. We got home all right."

Captain J.T. Percy, who also put down to refuel that same morning at Bordeaux in an Albatross aircraft, had perhaps the strangest flight of all. He took off that morning from Britain, bound for Lisbon and carrying only one passenger, a man in civilian clothes. When he landed into the Bordeaux hurly-burly and learned of the French capitulation, he was far from happy at having to proceed to Lisbon with a single passenger, feeling that it might mean the loss of the aircraft.

So when he was airborne he radioed to his base in Britain asking whether in view of the changed circumstances, he should turn for home, bringing as many evacuees as he could. To his astonishment he received the reply that he was to place himself and his aircraft under the orders of the passenger. He went aft to have a good look at this passenger who was thus invested with the most unusual powers. The passenger instructed him to go to Lisbon. When they reached Lisbon, the passenger told him to go on to Casablanca. When they arrived, the passenger said that Percy's job was to evacuate all the British engineers from French Morocco, lest that country should be attacked by the Italians. The mysterious passenger then disappeared and the captain never discovered who he was or whither he went. The majority of the engineers were taken, in several trips, to Lisbon, the remainder going by sea. Then Percy was told he could take the Albatross back to Britain. When he inquired how that was to be done, since the range of the aircraft necessitated a refuelling stop somewhere in France, he was told to solve that problem himself. He did so in the end by taking up the floorboards to get at the manholes of the petrol tanks. He filled up with petrol, and stacked the inside of the hull with more petrol in tins; his crew refuelled in flight through a funnel, and they brought the Albatross safely home to Britain.

During those same troubled days, the Empire flying-boat Cathay took off from Britain, carrying the Polish General Sikorski and a British liaison officer. Her pilot was Captain D.C.T. Bennett, who afterwards transferred to the RAF and, famous for his work with Bomber Command's Pathfinders, later held the rank of Air Vice-Marshal. Their destination was Biscarrosse, where General Sikorski had a rendezvous with the general staff of those formations of the Polish Army which were still fighting in France.

They alighted at Biscarrosse at about midday. A dinghy was put over the side and General Sikorski went ashore. Captain Bennett had pointed out the risks of delaying departure longer than a few hours, but the General had replied that he could not be ready to leave before five o'clock the following morning. Bennett was therefore faced by the problem of concealing for 17 hours a large, unarmed flying-boat on exposed waters liable to enemy bombardment at any moment, and towards the shores of which enemy troops were rapidly advancing. Before long, indeed, air bombardment of the area began with some severity. Afraid that Cathay might be sunk, he taxied her along the coast for about six miles, and ran her lightly aground on a sandy beach under cover of some trees, turning her violently as he did so, in order that she might come to rest facing open water.

The crew stayed there all that afternoon. A party of them went ashore, were fired on in the surrounding woods, and, when they telephoned to some French villagers nearby with the thought of getting more provisions, were warned to keep away as two tanks and some motor cyclists, the vanguard of the German forces, had just passed down the village street. They returned to the flying-boat and sat on board, listening to a distant rumble which they at last realised to be that of tanks on the move. Just before nightfall Captain Bennett started the engines, pulled Cathay off the beach, and taxied her back to her original moorings. They lay there all night, the crew taking it in turns to keep watch on the wings, but there were no incidents other than the incessant rumble of German armour, now close by.

Just before five o'clock in the morning General Sikorski returned, bringing with him his daughter, General Sosnowski and other officers of the Polish general staff. Cathay took off as quickly as possible, passing over a group of German tanks almost immediately after she was airborne. The

Polish officers were stationed at the windows of the flying-boat, to open fire on any enemy aircraft with whatever weapons they possessed. One or two enemy fighters did intercept them, but sheered off, doubtless owing to the resemblance of Cathay to the formidable RAF Sunderlands.

At one point, it seemed that they were to be pursued in earnest. Bennett managed to take refuge in a thick pall of black smoke drifting from some oil tanks burning on the French coast, and to shake off the pursuers. While still flying in this smoke, he calculated an estimated time of arrival at a point on the south coast of Britain which proved to be correct to the minute. Cathay brought the Polish staff safely to this country.

Towards the end of June the intensity of the air evacuation from France was over. Finished, for the moment, was most of the short-route work; there was a pause in the rhythm of merchant airways in a Britain which was preparing to withstand siege. The captains and crews were temporarily employed in a variety of tasks. Many of them were seconded to the Air Transport Auxiliary, and ferried fighting aircraft from factory to squadron.

Others of them, with the Ensign aircraft, were placed under the RAF Fighter Command, then preparing for the Battle of Britain. There were not at that time enough fighters to cover the whole of the south and east coasts of Britain; no matter how the squadrons were disposed, there were large gaps in the front through which enemy bomber squadrons might have penetrated freely, out of our fighters' range. It was necessary, therefore, working on all the indications that presented themselves and adding a little guess-work, to try to forecast which areas would be likely to receive the next attack by the Luftwaffe. Fighter squadrons were then rushed to airfields in that area, and with them flew the Ensigns, carrying the squadrons' nucleus ground staff, starting engines, ammunition and essential engineering gear. An Ensign might be stationed, for instance, with a fighter squadron which was urgently needed on the east coast of Scotland.

It was a matter of very few hours for it to arrive there, escorted by the fighters and carrying their necessary equipment and engineers. Often the margin was very narrow. Often they arrived and off-loaded just in time for the fighters to go up and engage the enemy overhead. As the strength of Fighter Command increased, it became less necessary to play this chess-game with the squadrons, and the Ensigns were gradually withdrawn. But the merchant air service can claim with pride to have played this ancillary part in the Battle of Britain itself.

Meanwhile the view of the airmen was turning more and more outward, on the long-distance routes. With the British Isles in a state of siege, the link of air transport with countries overseas became more vital than ever. There were great tasks to be accomplished, and urgently, on the routes to Africa and beyond, on the routes across the Atlantic to the arsenals of North America. Most of the available crews were soon absorbed into these enterprises. Speed and endurance combined became their aims, the distant lands their destinations.

CHAPTER 4

Within the British Isles

BEFORE THE WAR – and let us not blink this fact – the internal air services of Great Britain lagged behind standards that were being set elsewhere in the world. It was not the fault of the air line companies, who performed excellent service within their limited scope. Nor was it wholly the fault of geography and climate.

The lack of interest in air transport across Britain has often been excused by references to the short distances of travel, the excellence of rail and road competition, and the uncertainty of flying weather; but nevertheless, it is a fact that one of the busiest pre-war air lines of the world plied between New York and Boston, a distance comparable to that between London and Leeds, a route served by first-class railways and roads, and suffering the usual disadvantages of winter weather in a northern climate. British Islanders were not, on the whole, air-minded.

Still, there were healthy signs in Britain before the war. A number of internal routes had been well established. London was connected by daily air services with the midlands, the North Country and Scotland, with Northern Ireland and Eire, with the West Country and Wales, with the holiday resorts of the south coast. There were air links along the south coast. There were links between the big industrial cities of the north. The islands around the coast were linked to the mainland. The air services to the Channel Islands were particularly strengthened just before the war with the opening of Guernsey airport. Several of the air line companies extended their routes, during summer, to holiday resorts on the coasts or the near hinterlands of the Continent. The Orkneys, the Shetlands and the Hebrides were all served by air lines plying to the Scottish mainland.

Nor did Britain's air lines bear only the character of services to pleasure resorts for holiday-makers. Many of them were being used by men engaged in commerce. The mails were carried on the main routes.

Moreover, in the immediate pre-war period the air lines were being organised much more competently from a national point of view. The Air Transport Licensing Authority, set up in 1938, introduced some rationalisation into the air routes within the British Isles. The air line companies had formed themselves into the British Air Services Association to speak with one voice in matters of negotiation with the Government. The majority of the 81 light aeroplane clubs participated in a new scheme of financial assistance, which had as its object the establishment and training of the Civil Air Guard.

The whole system of ground organisation for flying had been revolutionised by the report of the Maybury Committee. This had recommended that the Government should provide and maintain a standard organisation, throughout the country, of radio facilities, weather information and air traffic control for all forms of civil aviation. This responsibility had been accepted by the Government, and the necessary organisation was being installed. Local authorities of many of the big towns and cities were realising more fully the benefits of air transport, and were constructing public airfields, municipally owned – there were 62 public and 43 private airfields licensed as "permanent" by 1939. The airports of London were being developed, with extensions to the landing area and navigational equipment at Croydon, and ambitious plans to increase the size of Heston. New airports serving London were projected – by the City of London at Fairlop and by the State at Lullingstone in Kent.

There was no doubt that in 1938 and 1939 the British Islanders were at last waking up to the value of commercial aviation in their own country. There is something of irony in the fact that, at that moment of awakening, ambitions and plans should be checked by the outbreak of war, the result of which was to depend so largely upon the air; something of hope in that the necessities of war should have proved the British to possess at least as great a skill as any people of the world in the construction and flying of aircraft.

It is not to be thought that the war obliterated the airmen who served the internal routes of Britain; they were far too valuable for that. The peacetime organisation ended abruptly with the Air Navigation (Restricted in Time of War) Order, which was promulgated on September 3rd, 1939, and which not only declared the eastern parts of England and Scotland to be prohibited areas to aircraft, but also forbade civil flying anywhere over the British Isles, without a special permit for each flight. All club and private flying was shut down for the duration of the war, but the air line companies were quickly organised for a highly valuable contribution to the general war effort.

Many of the captains who would otherwise have been called up from the reserve into the Forces were ordered to stay at their posts. Eighteen internal air line companies voluntarily placed their fleets, staffs and organisation at the disposal of the Air Minister. Arrangements were made for the Treasury to meet the cost of flying which these companies undertook by Air Ministry orders. And the whole thing was placed under the control of National Air Communications, as described in Chapter 2.

The men who had served the internal routes were allotted two chief tasks. The first was to assist in the air transport of RAF squadrons and supplies to

France (and later in their evacuation to Britain). The story of those days has already been told, but it should be emphasised that this task was shared by all the merchant air services of Britain. British Overseas Airways had the largest individual fleet of aircraft, but that Corporation was simply one unit of the many that National Air Communications controlled. Small air lines alike with large shared the honour of carrying supplies to the Forces in the 1940 battle area in France, and the fleets that flew back and forth across the Channel were made up of the airmen and aircraft of practically all the air lines of Britain.

The second task allotted to the internal air line companies was to continue to fly routes which were considered to be useful to the war effort. The principle upon which was decided which were the useful lines was simply that of common sense. Only those routes which were of definite value to the public and to the war effort were retained. It was clearly neither necessary nor desirable in wartime to have an air link between, for instance, the holiday resorts of Brighton and Bournemouth. On the other hand, when garrisons and RAF squadrons were stationed at such places as the Orkneys or the Shetlands, it was most important to maintain an air transport service to the mainland. The wartime routes served places separated from the mainland by water and inaccessible by rail or motor car, the alternative means of transport being by steamer services, in most cases infrequent and irregular. On these routes the aircraft carried the mail.

These were the chief routes, and the companies that flew them: the Channel Islands of Guernsey and Jersey were connected with each other, and with Shoreham airport on the south coast of England, by Jersey Airways Ltd. Great Western and Southern Air Lines Ltd. plied between Land's End and the Scilly Isles. The Isle of Man Air Services Ltd. flew between Liverpool and the Isle of Man, extending afterwards to Belfast. Railway Air Services Ltd. connected Glasgow, Belfast and Liverpool. West Coast Air Services Ltd., in co-operation with the Eireann Company, Aer Lingus Teoranta, resumed early in 1940 the service between Dublin and Liverpool, the eastern terminus later being transferred to Manchester. Two companies operated from Scotland. Allied Airways (Gandar Dower) Ltd. flew from Aberdeen to the Orkneys and the Shetlands. Scottish Airways Ltd. connected Inverness with the Orkneys and the Shetlands to the north; Glasgow with the islands of Islay, Tiree and the Hebrides to the west.

The English wartime terminal of the Channel Islands service was hastily transferred on June 18th, 1940, to Exeter, in order to give the aircraft shorter flights to and from Jersey and Guernsey. Jersey Airways Ltd. were working at full capacity to evacuate as many civilians as possible from the threatened Islands. Hundreds of evacuees were brought away who must otherwise have been left to the German occupation, for the steamers leaving the island were crowded to the rails. Other aircraft on their way back from France stopped at the Channel Islands when they could to lend a hand. But Jersey Airways bore the brunt of it.

Once France had fallen, and the last of the aircraft had landed in Britain from the Continent, the last ships had steamed from the French coast through bombardment to haven, the internal air routes of the British Isles were reorganised. National Air Communications, having served its purpose, ceased to exist. Many of the captains were transferred either temporarily or permanently to the Air Transport Auxiliary, that group of civil pilots who ferried RAF aircraft from the factories to the squadrons.

The internal air lines were no longer required to divert their aircraft at short notice to the tasks of military supply. They concentrated on the routes that crossed the sea, and were regrouped under an arrangement by which they agreed to fly the scheduled air services which the Air Ministry approved – services which had a basic usefulness in the war effort – under special financial arrangements.

Thus, as from June 27th, 1940, all the internal companies save one were grouped together, and managed by a committee, under the chairmanship of Sir Harold Hartley, called the Associated Airways Joint Committee. The company standing outside the group, but concluding a similar agreement with the Government, was Allied Airways (Gandar Dower) Ltd., which continued to fly services from Aberdeen to Kirkwall in the Orkneys and Sumburgh in the Shetlands.

Associated Airways Joint Committee set up its headquarters and its repair and overhaul unit on the civil airfield of Speke, outside Liverpool. The companies which were joined under the management of this committee were Railway Air Services Ltd., Air Commerce Ltd., Great Western and Southern Air Lines Ltd., Isle of Man Air Services Ltd., Scottish Airways Ltd., Western Isles Airways Ltd., and West Coast Air Services Ltd. Their operations were controlled and managed by Wing Commander A.H. Measures, with Captain G.P. Olley as his deputy.

The combined fleet of aircraft of which they disposed was not large. It consisted of 20 De Havilland aircraft – four D.H. 86s, fourteen D.H. 89s and two D.H. 84s. Four of these which had to be abandoned during the evacuation from France were later replaced by similar types. A fifth, a D.H. 84, was lost on services to the Scilly Islands. This aircraft, the property of Great Western and Southern Air Lines, took off from the Scilly Islands on June 3rd, 1941, carrying passengers. It did not reach Land's End. The likelihood is that it fell to the guns of a German fighter which was known to be in that neighbourhood at the time.

With this small fleet and with the most limited engineering facilities, the internal air lines of Britain commenced and continued to put up an astonishingly good performance. They operated regular services to Eire and Northern Ireland, the Scilly Isles, the Isle of Man, Islay, Tiree and the Hebrides, the Orkneys and the Shetlands. In spite of bad weather, their regularity was on the whole excellent. Day after day they plied between the islands and the mainland, carrying for the most part serving officers on duty or on leave, Government officials, the mails, and war freight to the outlying garrisons and squadrons. What load remained was available to paying passengers, for the most part business men, all engaged on vital work in the war effort, and using this swift means of communication to carry it out more efficiently.

As an instance of the pressure at which these small air lines were working, during the first year of its operation aircraft of the Associated Airways Joint Committee flew 1,226,590 miles, carrying 46,693 passengers, 889,898 lb. of mail and 227,332 lb. of freight. It would be idle to pretend that these were air transport operations on any considerable scale. But this much at least may fairly be said. These air line companies worked the few aircraft at their disposal with a regularity and to a capacity that can rarely have been equalled anywhere, even in peacetime; and the public demand for their services, often far greater than they could carry, suggested a healthy change in the general understanding in this country of the value of air travel over shorthaul routes.

There was another contribution which merchant airways made to the war effort at home, a contribution of considerable importance.

For many years before the war the two biggest British air lines employed a nucleus of ground engineers who had had as much experience in maintenance of aircraft engines and airframes as any similar group in the world. Some were withdrawn into the military aircraft industry when war broke out and played a notable part there, but others remained to continue their work of maintaining the merchant fleets of British Overseas Airways.

In the summer of 1940, when the very survival of Britain hung largely on the production of military aircraft for the R. A.F., the specialised knowledge of those engineers was called to help meet the national need. At the end of May, the Ministry of Aircraft Production asked British Overseas Airways to undertake the repair of military-aircraft engines. The shops at Croydon and Hythe were at once thrown open to the Ministry, the former to deal with land-planes, the latter with flying-boats. But this was only the start; much more could be done with more factory space.

So, on June 18th an advance party of engineers went down to the South Wales valleys, and took over a group of factory shops on the Treforest Trading Estate, near Cardiff, a relic of peacetime efforts to cure unemployment. They transferred the gear for overhauling aircraft engines from Croydon to Treforest, and set it up there within six days. Early in the following month a factory in full flow began to deliver overhauled engines to the RAF. By July 26th test-beds had been built in a field nearby, and the first engine was delivered off test.

While this engine factory had been getting under way in South Wales, others of the Corporation's ground staff had been rushed to Speke airfield, near Liverpool, to begin assembling for the RAF American fighter and reconnaissance aircraft which were reaching this country in crates, by sea. Shortly afterwards the work at Speke was taken over by American engineers. The British staff were withdrawn, and within three days had started on similar work in a factory in the West of England, putting out a production of two aircraft a day within three weeks. These were only emergency measures, and in time RAF engineers were able to take over the whole of the work. The Airways engineers were then concentrated on two shops that had been opened in Bath, one in a former garage, and one in a printing works, for the repair of twisted and damaged aircraft propellers.

From that time onwards, British Overseas Airways carried out its engineering work for the RAF at the Treforest factory, and at the propeller shops in Bath. The whole thing was grouped into an administrative unit called the Propeller and Engine Repair Auxiliary, under the control at various times of Mr. A.J. Quin-Harkin and Mr. J.H. Robson. The Treforest factory was in charge of Mr. G.A. Hummerstone.

This Treforest factory was scattered through 13 shops at the foot of the Rhondda valley, under the shadow of pitwheels, powerhouses and the greenness of the Welsh hills. The engines for repair and overhaul arrived for the most part at a railway siding in the factory itself. In the first shops they were stripped down to the smallest component, each engine being kept on a separate moving trolley, each part being most carefully checked and tested, sent forward for rejection or repair. The overhauled components went into big storage bays stretching the length of the shop; thence they travelled out to the various sub-assembly shops, completely new engines being built around each overhauled crank-case.

Once the reconstructed engines, sprucely painted and smart, emerged from the factory they were hauled to the roaring test-beds a mile or so up into the hills, and set in motion on the concrete stands, around which men worked in a half-lit pandemonium of noise. When they had passed all the tests, the engines were sent back to the RAF, into battle.

One of the shops at Treforest was particularly interesting. Peacetime airways in Britain, with the manufacturers at their backs, had not attempted to salvage spare parts from badly damaged engines. In wartime, however, it was a very different case. At one time the bottleneck of the whole aircraft production of the country was the dearth of spare parts. The Airways engineers therefore suggested – they were the pioneers of this in Britain

– that engines which had been so badly damaged in action or in crashes as to seem worth nothing but the melting-pot, should be sent to Treforest to see what could be extracted from them. One shop was set aside for this purpose, and to it the damaged engines came – battered, bullet-scarred, smothered in dirt, seared by fire. Experts examined them, cut them open with oxy-acetylene, and stripped them down to their smallest components, cleansing and testing each part, reclaiming from the wreck an amazing quantity of perfectly good spares.

It was calculated that, over a period of a year, when the cost of running this shop had been taken into account, the profit of this department alone at the cost price of 35 of the main items salved was equivalent to £120,000. But in the early days the value of such work could not be measured in terms of money. The country's aircraft output had, at times, been held up for the lack of even such small items as nuts and bolts of the right pattern; spare parts for American aircraft were of particular value. The work in that shop at Treforest meant, not £120,000, but more RAF aircraft in the air, fighting the battle for survival.

The success of this factory at Treforest was due primarily to the deep knowledge, acquired with diligence over many years, of the nucleus of Airways engineers. An instance will demonstrate that skill. Once, early in their history, they were sent eight battered and damaged engines from Heinkel seaplanes of the Luftwaffe which had been shot down in Britain; they were asked to produce from this wreckage one, or if possible more than one workable engine. They did not know exactly how the Heinkel engines worked, and they had to reach that knowledge largely by theory, for all engines were too badly damaged even to be turned over by hand. With patience and care they stripped them all down, and eventually produced five complete engines in full working order.

But the skill of these comparatively few engineers could not possibly produce the big output which Treforest reached. That was achieved by building up round them a skilled factory staff recruited from men and women who had no experience of aircraft engineering at all, and most of whom had no factory experience of any kind. Many of the men were former miners, medically unfit for work in the pits. They proved first-class at skilled factory work. It may be, indeed, that the post-war legacy of this wartime factory will be a body of skilled mechanics available in what was once a distressed area of South Wales.

The women – they recruited hundreds of them – proved as good as the men. They were recruited from all kinds of occupations, shop assistants, clerks, domestic servants, housewives, cooks, and so on. They came with a will, young and old. At one of the benches, for instance, was to be found a miner's widow who at one time had three sons in the Forces – one a soldier missing in Malaya, one fighting in North Africa, one a parachutist – and 20 grandchildren of whom the oldest had already entered the Merchant Navy. These women were not performing merely routine tasks in the factory; some of them rose to positions of responsibility. And responsibility it truly is, when one works on an aircraft engine that is going back into battle carrying an air crew behind it. The most treasured possessions of that factory are letters from RAF squadrons asking to be supplied with overhauled engines from Treforest.

The two propeller-repair factories at Bath were also built up on a nucleus, not more than half a dozen, of skilled mechanics and engineers from merchant airways of peacetime. In those quiet workshops the propellers that had been bent and twisted in combat or in crash were meticulously straightened, sometimes after annealing in electric furnaces at a temperature of 400 degrees Centigrade; then balanced once more on the hubs with such delicacy that a bluebottle alighting on the tip of a blade would set the whole propeller in motion.

Into these factories, too, many women were drawn – countrywomen and townswomen, housewives and domestic servants, women who had always toiled and women who never before had seen the inside of a factory. They proved equally successful. In these factories some of the jobs of greatest responsibility were held by women. Ask any of them how they sustained their toil, and they will reply it was by the knowledge that it contributed to British air supremacy. Ask the factory manager about the spirit of the people who worked there, and he will tell you of one quiet girl whose home was wrecked during a blitz on Bath which also damaged one of the propeller factories. She reported for duty on time next morning, and although she had nowhere to live, she worked every day of the next week until 10 p.m., helping largely to get the factory into production again within a few days. That, he will say, was typical of all.

PART II

THE EMPIRE AIR ROUTES

Short S.33 C-class Empire Flying Boat, G-AFRA *Cleopatra* of BOAC, circling Durban, South Africa, prior to landing on the harbour after flying the 'Horseshoe Route' from Sydney.

CHAPTER 5

The Links in the Chain

THE PERSON WHO reads this book in an armchair by his or her fireside must read now not with his eyes only, but with his imagination. The outlines of his room the familiar things about him must dissolve, regrouping themselves into the image of bright sunlight on some distant stretch of water, a strip of yellow beach and palm-trees, the blueness of hills beyond, a power-launch rocking gently on the swell; one of the crew – a native – far keener of eyesight than the English coxswain, is the first to spot the tiny insect droning steadily over the hill-tops, rapidly approaching until all can discern the graceful outline of a flying-boat, the upward curve of its prow like the breast-stroke of a powerful swimmer; the port wing dips into a wide circle, straightens again into a clean, direct approach; the hull lingers for a moment just clear of the water touches down with a vivid, sharp arrow of white foam, glides majestically to a stop, the wake rushing out behind it as the launch speeds towards the mooring-buoy. This is the alighting of a flying-boat at any one of the scores of halting-places on the far-stretched chain of the Empire air routes.

Of all the routes which British airmen fly, these are the most inspiring to the mind. Little more than a decade ago only fragments of them existed. By 1939 most of them were established, and the last links of the chain were forged during the early days of the war itself – the aerial chain connecting Britain with all the chief countries of the British Commonwealth. The size of this achievement cannot be truly measured until it is understood that the airmen worked against all the navigational difficulties inherent in wartime, and that their tools, the aircraft, were too few in number and often obsolescent in quality (as indeed some still are).

That chain was forged primarily by the endurance and skill of the airmen themselves. Where it passed through a zone of battle they took no account of the risk. When it was broken by armed force, as it was several times, they knitted it together again over some different route. By their endeavours they maintained air communication between the British countries of the world, vital as it was in wartime, and still more vital as it may prove to be in times of peace.

At the end of August 1939 the main Empire routes were these: Twice a week flying-boats plied between Britain and South Africa (Southampton

A pilot leans out of a cockpit window on *Cleopatra*. *Cleopatra* was the last C-class Empire flying boat to be built and was handed over to BOAC in May 1940. Some sources identify this individual as Captain James Peers.

and Durban), a journey of four and a half days. A third service each week ran between England and Kisumu, a neat little town built round the end of a U-shaped bay on the shores of Lake Victoria, in Kenya, beneath the frown of a semi-circle of mountains capped with rain.

From these main African routes there was a weekly connection across Central Africa to the west coast. It flew from the desert heat of Khartoum across scrub-land and equatorial jungle to Lagos, on the coast of Nigeria, whence Elders Colonial Airways Ltd. continued it to Takoradi on the Gold Coast. Southampton to Takoradi by this route occupied four and a half days.

Three times a week flying-boats took off from Southampton for Singapore, whence Qantas Empire Airways carried the load on to Sydney, Australia. It took nine and a half days to reach Sydney from Southampton.

At Bangkok in Siam a twice-weekly branch service of D.H. 86 aircraft flew across French Indo-China to Hong Kong. It took the traveller from England five and a half days to arrive at Hong Kong.

Flying-boats ran a twice-weekly service from Southampton to Karachi, India, whence, in association with Indian Trans-Continental Airways, Atalanta-class land-planes carried the service through to Calcutta. Passengers reached Calcutta four days after leaving Southampton.

All these Empire trunk routes were flown nominally by Imperial Airways Ltd., although that company had already, in effect, become part of the British Overseas Airways Corporation.

The only great Dominions which the Empire routes did not then fully

The 'End of the Chain'. The Short S.30 Empire-class flying boat *Aotearoa*, seen here, was sent out from Britain to open the route between Australia and New Zealand.

serve were Canada and New Zealand. The Atlantic experiment had already begun, although it had not yet reached the stage of carrying passengers; its story must be told later in this account, together with that of all the Atlantic routes. The link to New Zealand had been planned before war broke out – planned, indeed, as the first stage of a great new air route from Australia and New Zealand across the Pacific Ocean to Canada, thus completing the British air circuit of the globe. The war meant the postponement of that ambition, but the link between Australia and New Zealand was made as quickly as possible, and it connected in New Zealand with the trans-Pacific route opened by Pan-American Airways.

Early in 1940 was formed Tasman Empire Airways Ltd., a joint concern composed of British Overseas Airways, Qantas Empire Airways and Union Airways of New Zealand, to operate the flying-boat route between Sydney and Auckland.

Captain J.W. Burgess opened the route on April 30th, 1940, in the Empire flying-boat Aotearoa, which had been sent out from Britain. Watched by a big crowd, and with some ceremony, he took off from Auckland and made an uneventful flight to Sydney. Another flying-boat from Britain, Awarua, enabled the service to be flown once weekly, and soon thrice fortnightly. The link has held ever since. But it should not be imagined that this is an easy route to fly, Captain Burgess himself describes the weather over the Tasman Sea as some of the worst he has met over any ocean in the world. To the south lies a vast mass of ocean leading to Antarctica, from which no weather reports are available, and in wartime there is nothing from even the few ships which cross the Tasman.

The first phase of the war, up to the German invasion of France, did little to disrupt the long Empire air routes which have been sketched above, although their first stages all ran from Britain across France, Italy, Greece, and the Mediterranean to Egypt. Only three days after the declaration of war the Air Officer Commanding, Egypt, put in an urgent plea for a merchant land-plane service between Egypt and Britain, to carry important documents and Government officials.

The request was quickly met. Land-planes were put on to the new route, which ran from Shoreham in Sussex, through Bordeaux and Marseilles to Tunis and Malta, thence to Alexandria via Sollum. On September 22nd, 1940, Fortuna, Captain A.C.P. Johnson, left Shoreham to start the service. It was not long before it had been extended eastwards to India. The service continued to operate twice weekly until Italy's declaration of war blocked the Mediterranean air. There was one accident. A Lockheed which took off from Sollum, on the Western Desert coast, homeward-bound on December 21st, 1939, failed to arrive on time at Malta. It had come down in the sea 200 miles from the Maltese coast, close to a small sailing ship, being forced to that risk in spite of a strong wind and a rough sea. Two members of the crew and three passengers were drowned; the remainder were rescued by the sailing ship.

There was another incident at the far eastern end of the Empire routes which might have been as distressing, but which ended more happily. On November 8th, 1939, the D.H.86 aircraft Dardanus, Captain J.N. Wilson, an Australian, was flying with three passengers from Hong Kong to Bangkok. As they were passing the island of Wai Chao, Dardanus was suddenly attacked by three Japanese fighters – Japan was not then, of course, at war with Great Britain. The aircraft was riddled – 92 bullet-holes were later counted – but none of the crew or passengers was hurt, and Captain Wilson most skilfully put down on the island. The passengers were at once sent back to Hong Kong, but the crew were held for more than a week before they were released. Dardanus was eventually flown out and repaired. The Japanese brusquely refused any apology or compensation, saying that the aircraft had flown too close to Wai Chao, which they regarded as one of their fortified bases.

These things apart, the Empire routes were flown smoothly and steadily during the early months of the war. Most remarkable at that time along the routes was a feat, not of flying but of salvage.

When war broke over Europe, a party of British aircraft engineers must have been among the Englishmen most remote from conflict. They were living in huts of planks and thatch on the banks of a remote river in the heart of Central Africa, toiling at the hull of a flying-boat that lay damaged on the swampy river-bank.

She was the Imperial Airways flying-boat *Corsair*. In March 1939, homeward bound from Durban, she had been forced off course over the Belgian Congo by exceptionally bad weather. Running short of fuel, the captain saw beneath him a small patch of fairly straight water, upon which he managed to alight; but before he could stay Corsair's run, she collided with a muddy bank, stove a hole in her hull, and sank in a few feet of water. Nobody was hurt and all the mail was salvaged by cutting a hole in the top of the hull. There remained only the weary process of repairing her and getting her into the air again.

Corsair lay at Faraje – though it is not clear why so desolate a spot should ever have been dignified with a name – on the river Dangu. All around her lay scrubland, marsh and swamp; even the nearest native village was some miles distant. A party of engineers was flown out to a point in Africa some 200 miles from Faraje, completing the journey at first by road, then on foot over the swamp. There they worked in an atmosphere almost as humid as it was hot, constructing a rudimentary dry dock around *Corsair's* hull, slipping a cradle under her and, with the help of scores of locals, hauling her on ropes to firm ground. They repaired her hull and her roof and launched her again, ready for take-off. By this time it was July.

The 'Plane that Built a Village'. When *Corsair* crash-landed in the remote Belgian Congo, locals toiled for nine months to get her airborne again. She left behind a new village, Corsairville.

The take-off presented grave problems. The stretch of river, swollen as it was by the rainy season, was still far too narrow and short, and half-way along its length it took a dangerous bend. Locals were employed to cut down all the trees and rushes along both banks, to allow passage for Corsair's wings. A large stake was then driven into the bank, and the tail of the flying-boat warped to it. Thus secured, her engines were started and advanced to full power; when they were roaring, the tie-rope was slipped and Corsair sped at full throttle over the water. She swerved a little at the bend, the captain realised that she would not get off in time. He cut the engines. She slowed down on the water, and came against a large protruding rock, which stove another hole in her hull. Months of work had gone for nothing; the whole weary process had to be started again.

She was hauled on to firm ground once more, the hull repaired a second time. By now war had begun and it had become more urgent than ever to return Corsair to the regular routes. But the dry season had started, the river had shrunk, and there would not be enough water for another take-off attempt for several months. Captain J.C. Kelly Rogers, who had then taken charge of the salvage operations, decided that, sooner than wait for rain, he would build a dam clear across the river Dangu and create an artificial lake.

They built a village by the riverside to house the native labour that was necessary, and cut a road through the swamp to the site of the proposed dam. They hauled timber from a distance of 30 miles, drove a double, buttressed palisade across the river-bed, and filled the hollows with stones and mud cut from anthills. At last the water had risen sufficiently far up the depth-board they had planted in the middle of the river, and all the submerged rocks had been marked; they were ready for take-off. Once again Corsair's tail was warped to a large stake ashore to restrain her until the engines had reached full power. Captain Rogers took her controls, and through the early morning mist of January 6th, 1940, lifted her from the patch of water upon which she had lain for nine months, circled once to dip a salute to the river Dangu, and brought her back to her war job on the Empire routes. Since then Corsair has flown considerably more than half a million miles, carrying hundreds of tons of vital supplies over the war routes, and many Allied passengers of importance. She is flying yet.

In Central Africa there is a memento of those nine months of toil. At Faraje, on the Dangu river, there stands the new mud village built for the native labourers. It is named Corsairville.

CHAPTER 6

Horseshoe to Australia

ITALY DECLARED WAR on June 10th, 1940. Just as that declaration, by bringing enemy air power to the shores of the Mediterranean, closed that sea to our shipping save in the most urgent circumstances, so for a time it cut the air route. This was the first serious break in the chain of our air communications since the start of the war; and truly serious it was. The routes in Africa, India, Australia and New Zealand all converged to a multiple, thick strand which stretched across Italy and France to the British Isles, and that was the strand which had been cut. The very engineering bases upon which some of them depended were stationed in England; spare parts and new engines all originated there, the central organisation was there.

The distant routes resembled the healthy arteries of a body in which the artery connecting them to the heart had been severed. More serious yet was the position in Britain. The siege was fast closing around her shores; British forces overseas, notably in Egypt and East Africa, were preparing to withstand an assault, the power of which could not then be gauged; the loyal Dominions were squaring grimly for the struggle. At that moment when swift lines of communication through the air were most essential, it seemed as though they were to be denied to Britain and her scattered Allies and formations.

Now the Italian declaration of war had always been a possibility, and plans had been laid long before to rearrange the Empire routes to meet it. It had been decided to swing the flying-boats away from Europe altogether, and to run them back and forth along a great horseshoe-shaped route with its extremities resting on Durban in the west and Sydney in the east; the horseshoe curved through East and Central Africa to Khartoum and Cairo, thence via the Empire route through Palestine, Iraq, the Persian Gulf, India, Burma, Siam, and Singapore to Australia. In other words, the two former Empire routes from Britain to Durban and to Sydney were to be joined together at Cairo, and the European section was to be cut away altogether.

The plan, agreed with the French, intended to replace that severed section by a land-plane link from Britain, through France and the French North African territory, across the Sahara Desert to Northern Nigeria, and thence onwards to Khartoum.

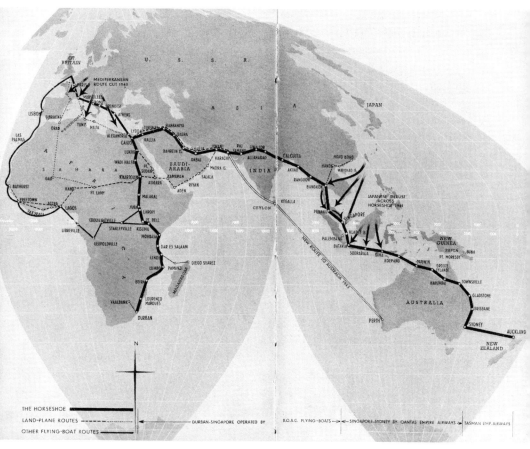

'The Horseshoe'. This map is centred on the two continental meridians of Africa and Australia, so that a more accurate impression may be given of the relative distances along the routes.

To make that plan quite clear: the flying-boats were to ply back and forth on a long Horseshoe Section, linking 16 countries between Durban and Sydney; the Horseshoe Section was to be linked with Britain by a land-plane service across the Sahara Desert.

The first part of the plan went splendidly – was already in train when the Italians declared war. The first essential was to establish a new engineering base for the flying-boats on the Horseshoe Section itself. Durban had been chosen as the site at one end of the route, to share the work with the engineering shops already established by Qantas Empire Airways at Sydney, at the other.

When Italy declared war the first two parties of ground engineers, together with their equipment, were already five days out from Southampton, bound for Durban by sea; the rest were to embark two days later. Two men who had been sent ahead to supervise the construction of the new base were southbound in a flying-boat, beyond Athens, past the danger area. By mid-June these two had arrived in Durban, and were already re-arranging the marine airport there for the burden that was to be placed upon it, and renting an old warehouse for conversion into an engine overhaul shop. By June 19th, only nine days after Italy entered the war, the Horseshoe Section was in operation with a weekly service from either end.

By the end of June the first two main engineering parties and equipment had arrived by sea. In six weeks the base was sufficiently established to allow the Horseshoe Section service to be duplicated. It is difficult to imagine quicker work than that.

The flying-boats themselves were variously disposed on June 10th. Sixteen of the fleet were on service east or south of Alexandria, and were able, therefore, to switch at once to the new arrangement. Three more were in the Mediterranean area, having been instructed to avoid all Italian territory and to fly via Malta and Navarino, on the Greek coast. Of these, Cathay was at Ajaccio, homeward-bound, and proceeded safely to Britain; Caledonia was at Corfu, in the Ionian islands, and proceeded outward-bound to join the Horseshoe fleet; Clyde was at Malta, homeward-bound with a party of RAF officers, including Air Chief Marshal Sir Robert Brooke-Popham.

Although Italy lay between them and home, the captain agreed to their request to make for Britain next morning. Just before take-off, in the early hours of June 11th, it was discovered that one of her engines was giving only half-power, and there seemed no time to set it right as the general anticipation was a heavy raid from the Italian coast only 60 miles distant. There was a heavy swell outside the bay which would almost inevitably overturn the flying-boat if, as was quite likely with an exceptional load and a faulty engine, she were not airborne before reaching the open sea. Her captain therefore taxied her out through the entrance of the bay until the swell began to toss her, then swung her right round and drove hard, back into the bay and towards the rugged cliffs of the coast. She came off with only 200 feet of water to spare. Off Pantelleria she passed over two Italian torpedo-boats, and a little later over two enemy submarines. Otherwise the journey home was without incident.

Meanwhile the men of the Airways ground staffs had to be withdrawn hastily from the areas of new hostility. The Rome staff left on the Embassy train, having been granted diplomatic recognition. Those at Tunis and Malta retired temporarily to Algiers. The two men remaining at Brindisi had an hour's notice to board the last flying-boat through Italy, being sped on their way to Athens by the tears and kisses of the lamenting Italian staff at the airport. There they collected the families from Greece and Crete and made the long journey by train and road through Turkey, Syria and Palestine to

Egypt. In spite of the complexities of this sudden withdrawal from an old-established route, all the men and equipment of the merchant air service were brought safely away with the exception of one aircraft engine and a few odd spare parts.

It will be remembered that the plan for re-arranging the Empire routes envisaged a Horseshoe Section of flying-boats linked to Britain by a land-plane service across the Sahara. The Horseshoe Section was established much faster than had been thought possible. Not so the Sahara route. The Italian entry into the war could be foreseen and planned against; nobody could have foretold the collapse of France.

This Sahara route had been regarded as a reserve for the Lockheed aircraft which had been plying between Britain and Egypt via the Mediterranean. The first of them left England on June 15th, crossing to the North African coast at Oran. At that point the captain was faced by nearly 2,000 miles of probably the worst desert in the world, the Sahara. He flew in a south-south-easterly direction towards Lake Chad, and the rough airfield at Fort Lamy, in the French territory just over the north-eastern border of Nigeria. He flew hour after hour over nothing but a waste of sand and rock, relieved occasionally by patches of camelthorn. There was a small airfield at Gao at which he refuelled. Then he flew on to Fort Lamy and through to the Sudan and Egypt.

Just before the capitulation of France, Lothair also flew from England to Cairo over the Sahara, and soon afterwards Lafayette made the journey in the other direction. It had to fly via Kano, in Nigeria, and Lisbon. There were not to be many more Sahara flights. On June 28th a ban was placed on flying over French colonial territory. That was the end of the Sahara route. The British Isles were cut off from the Empire routes altogether. The only merchant air links between besieged Britain and the outside world ran between Scotland and Sweden, Liverpool and Dublin, Poole and Lisbon; this last, re-established by the flying-boats Champion and Cathay, to connect with the transatlantic Clipper service of Pan-American Airways.

Nevertheless, the flying-boats were fully established on the Horseshoe Section between Durban and Sydney. This route, though it was shortened later by the Japanese, played a vital role, as Air Chief Marshal Tedder himself stated, in the communications that lay behind our Middle East campaigns. It merits a description.

The flying-boat takes off at first morning-light from Congella, the airport at the head of the land-locked harbour of the modern city of Durban – from a basin surrounded by docks, ships loading, cranes and gantries, headed by the big concrete apron of the flying-boat base, with the hangars and work-shops of the engineers crowded closely behind.

The first part of the flight follows the surf of the east coastline of Africa, the hills inshore green with sugar plantations, the beach a strip of perpetual yellow, overlooked by pleasant villas snuggled into the cliffs. There are two refuelling stops on the first day, in the Portuguese harbours of Beira and Lourenço Marques, the former blazing with the scarlet of flamboyant trees in the noonday sun, the latter an expanse of grey-green, choppy sea, across which launches carry the passengers to lunch in a restaurant built on a pontoon under the shadow of a tall dock-side crane. By evening the flying-boat is circling the long, thin island of Mozambique, its white houses crowded around the medieval fort, and alights at the village of Lumbo, opposite on the mainland.

Crew and passengers spend the night there in the Hotel do Lumbo, which British Overseas Airways has hired from the Portuguese, a romantic building some 600 years old of thick mud walls which are as serviceable as ever. Originally it was the centre of the local slave trade; the traders lived where the restaurant and lounges now occupy the first floor, and the shackled slaves were collected in dungeons below – now finely decorated bedrooms and white-tiled bathrooms. During the last war it was the headquarters of the local British troops, who fought a battle through the village street with forces from a German troopship which ran aground a little farther down the coast.

It is doubtful if even the slaves of olden times rose quite so early as do the passengers the following day, for take-off is before dawn, a long flight lies ahead. There is a brief halt at Lindi at the south-east tip of Tanganyika, another at Dar es Salaam, that pretty little European town capped by two church spires, on the shores of a tranquil, tropical harbour; as they sip ginger ale on a shaded balcony overlooking the alighting area, passengers' survey souvenirs of the last war and of this. Protruding from the water are the wrecks of a ship and dry dock with which the Germans tried to block the harbour mouth nearly 30 years ago, when Tanganyika was their colony. And on the opposite shore stands a square grey building, nominally the abode of the German Lutheran Mission, which was found to be a centre of espionage during this war, and to contain a shrine to Hitler – a large mural of him beneath which devotees kept candles always burning, and knelt in Aryan adoration.

The flying-boat takes off within the hour for the palm-fringed, extremely hot, busy naval port at Mombasa on the coast of Kenya. Thence she strikes inland, climbing high over the mountains. If the clouds are kind, the passengers can see, away to port, the double peak of the greatest mountain in Africa, Kilimanjaro, rising from a base of white cloud to a height of 19,300 feet; firm and graceful stands Kilimanjaro in outline, a white skirt of cloud at its waist, a ruffle of light cloud around its neck, and on its rounded dome of a forehead a lace cap of snow.

There are thunderstorms rolling about these skies, to be dodged before the flying-boat alights at the neat town of Kisumu on the tip of Lake Victoria, where potting at crocodile and hippo, or sitting on a cape to watch the glory of sunset over the lake are the local recreations. From there a short flight into the evening leads to Port Bell, farther round the lake into Uganda, a few miles north of the equator. A drive follows in an elderly motor bus, through small villages set in banana plantations, along a road that dips and curves over pleasant hills, past groups of sturdy, attractive natives, the women wearing long drapes of brilliantly coloured cloth, from shoulder to ankle, looking for all the world as though they were in full evening dress; and so to Kampala, the capital, for the night.

In the luxury of the hotel at Kampala – that trimmest of towns, where the municipality not only employs hundreds of lawn-mowers on the public grass, but cuts, compulsorily and at public expense, every man's private front hedge – the passengers listen perhaps to some of the queer animal-stories told by the airways ground staff who live on the shores of this equatorial lake. They hear how the hippo lie idly on the surface, watching the flying-boats descend and diving deeply only at the moment of touch-down; they hear of crocodile which ate pieces of the red rubber mooring-buoys, until metal had to be substituted.

Best of all the stories is that of the crocodile Lutembe, said to be about 200 years old, a repulsive fellow, covered with ticks and almost toothless. When a local resident goes down to the lake-shore by the flying-boat station and calls "Lutembe," the crocodile comes swimming ashore in answer to his name (so tame that men have sat astride his back) to be rewarded by a lump of rotten meat. Lutembe is said to have acquired this habit in earlier times, when the local tribe summoned him to dispose of prisoners-of-war whom they cast into the water. Lately he has been bringing a young crocodile with him when he answers to his name, and the natives are convinced that Lutembe, aware of his old age and the imminence of death, is training up a young friend to succeed him in this lucrative sinecure.

On the way down to the lake, early in the morning of the third day of the journey, the captain grumbles at the long, hard grind ahead of him in taking-off the flying-boat from such placid waters at such an altitude. Once off, she heads almost due north towards Laropi on the upper waters of the White Nile. If conditions are favourable the captain may divert her a little to fly low over the Murchison Falls, where all the waters of the Victoria Nile race through a gorge only 19 feet wide, and where large numbers of elephant, rhino and buck shy away into the bush from the swift shadow of the aircraft, and hippo and crocodile in hundreds plunge from slimy mud-banks into deeper water.

All this part of Africa is a tenement-house of big game. North of Laropi, following the course of the Nile past Juba, the flying-boat may pass low over part of the famous Bor herd of elephant – elephant who have been inspected from the air so often that they have grown sophisticated, merely glancing up from the tall grasses in which they are feeding, to murmur something about "another of those flying-boats," and to continue with their occupation, while a flock of white birds hovers and swoops around their backs.

The next stop is a straight stretch of the White Nile at Malakal, encompassed by desert heat, where the flying-boat comes to rest opposite a riverside village of the Shilluk tribe – locals of remarkable tallness who stand one-legged surveying the scene, the other foot resting on the knee, or paddle smilingly in dugout canoes towards the launches so that one may see the intricate, mud-woven patterns of their hair. By teatime, having circled the confluence of the White and Blue Niles, the passengers are resting in the shade of an hotel terrace at Khartoum, drinking iced coffee from large glass jugs and lazily regarding the passing of the curved sails of a felucca.

The fourth day's flight follows the Nile to Cairo, touching down at Wadi Haifa, most decorous of riverside villages where the Airways' halt is that long, low house built by Gordon and used by Kitchener as a headquarters during his river war; and then among the solemn antiquity of the temples at Luxor.

Cairo is the Near East regional centre of British Overseas Airways. The flying-boats alight by a houseboat on the Nile at Rod-el-Farag, sweeping over the famous club-island of Gezira and disembarking passengers on the northern outskirts of this ancient-and-modern city, filled during wartime with khaki. The fifth day's flight heads north-east over the rich green patterns of the Delta fields, then over the Suez Canal and the Sinai desert, to Tiberias on the Sea of Galilee (in the early days of the war), and now Kallia, on the shores of the Dead Sea. Now the journey is moving along that great desert belt which separates airmen of Britain from all the southerly Dominions with which their routes must link. It is weary flying over the duns and browns of the Syrian desert, relieved only by the straight thread of the oil pipeline; equally weary, after a halt on Lake Habbaniya, near Baghdad, over the desert that stretches from there to Basra, at the head of the Persian Gulf.

The marine airport at Basra, on the waters where the Tigris and Euphrates rivers join, lies alongside the land airfield, with a big hotel between to serve both. Before dawn on the sixth day, to the light of a river flarepath, the flying-boat skims past the wharves and the ships that lie discharging cargo, and heads down the Gulf, alighting for breakfast at daybreak by a long jetty protruding from the island of Bahrain, traditional centre of the pearl-fishing industry and probably destined to be one of the most important merchant air stations in the world. The notorious heat of the Persian Gulf is not felt in flight, not until the flying-boat alights to refuel at Dubai, close by the old Arab fort of Sharjah, remote from the world, and from anything but sand, heat and flies. The next halt is another desert station, at Jiwani on the Baluchistan coast of the Arabian Sea, shortly after leaving which the flying-boat passes that curious rock formation by the shore which has already been described in resemblance to the skyline of some such skyscraper-city as New York. At the end of the day is the marine airport of Karachi, aerial gateway to India, in a setting of docks, wharves and ocean ships, and customs and immigration formalities of extreme intricacy and length.

A flight clear across northern India occupies the eighth day, from Karachi to Calcutta. On this section of the route the airports and traffic are handled by Indian National Airways, who assist British Overseas Airways. Alight on the sacred lake of Raj Samand on a feast day – Raj Samand with its unpolluted waters and the white, fairy-book palaces and terraces of its shores – and there will be men waiting to hang around passengers' necks garlands of roses and jasmine, while faintly across the lake hums the melody of an Indian song.

Forward from there to the other sacred lake of Mahdo Sagar, in Gwalior, formed by an irrigation dam across the neck of some hills, and the airways junction for Delhi. The lake is fed in the season by most severe rains that wash away roads and bridges, sometimes placing swollen torrents between intending passengers and their flying-boat. (There is a story of three British officers, homeward-bound, who were confronted by such a problem, and who solved it by swimming fully clothed a river in flood in order to catch the aircraft for home.)

There is but one more halt, on the broad waters of the Ganges river at Allahabad; then, by evening, the flying-boat is dropping down over the Willingdon Bridge, passing by an Indian temple, to alight on the Hooghly river, at the airport of Bally for Calcutta.

From sprawling, crowded, odorous Calcutta the journey continued down the Bay of Bengal to Rangoon in Burma, to Bangkok in Siam, and thus to Singapore, whence the crews of Qantas Empire Airways continued through the vividness of the East Indies to their own country of Australia, to the ocean port of Sydney, New South Wales.

That, in the days when it was first established after the Italian declaration of war, was the Horseshoe Section into which the Empire air routes had been swung.

CHAPTER 7

'Clyde' to the Congo

THERE WAS ANOTHER, smaller Empire route which was interrupted, first by the Italian declaration of war and then by the collapse of France – the land-plane route across Central Africa connecting the West Coast with Egypt. With the air communications to Britain cut, it was vital that this route should be reopened and increased to its greatest capacity. The need, of course, was for the swiftest possible link between the British Isles and the Middle East Forces, to whom the sea route round the Cape of Good Hope meant a voyage of 12,000 miles. It was imperative that, at the least, official documents should be able to travel between London and Cairo much more rapidly. Fortunately, much had already been done in pioneering the trans-African route, as the following facts will show.

The first survey flight of this trans-African route was made by the RAF in 1925, under the command of Squadron Leader (later Air Marshal Sir) Arthur Coningham, from Khartoum in the Sudan to Kano in Nigeria. In

'The long way round'. Captain and co-pilot at the controls of a C-class Empire flying-boat. With the Mediterranean route cut, these were the aircraft that came down the west coast to the Congo, to link Great Britain with the Middle East.

The flying boat base at Kisumu, Kenya, pictured just before the outbreak of war. Note the flying-boat runway in foreground. (US Library of Congress)

1930 a further RAF survey flight travelled beyond Kano to Bathurst, in the Gambia, on the African West Coast. Between 1930 and 1935 the airfields of the route were built – at El Geneina, El Fasher and El Obeid in the Sudan, and at Kano and Maiduguri in Nigeria. They were built by the Colonial Governments concerned, and financed either by them or by the British Government. In 1936 Imperial Airways opened a regular merchant air line over the route from Lagos on the Nigerian coast, through Kano and Khartoum, up the valley of the Nile to Cairo. Imperial Airways (later British Overseas Airways) continued to fly that route after war began.

The men who organised the ground services did so in most difficult tropical conditions, improvising a great deal at first but soon providing facilities which, although not elaborate, were perfectly adequate for a once-weekly air service across one of the remotest parts of the world. One story will perhaps indicate the nature of the countries over which this air route was stretched. When the airfield was completed outside the ancient walled city of Kano, and the first D.H.86 of the Imperial Airways fleet arrived to open the regular service in 1936, the Emir held a ceremonial parade of his soldiers at the airfield, which was lined by his footguards. The aircraft took off on a short flight, carrying an official party.

As it landed again, and the passengers stepped out, they were treated to the "jafi," a ceremony which has lived on in Kano for centuries, and nowhere else in the world. Charging across the airfield straight towards them came about a hundred of the Emir's horseguards, clad in full chain-mail which was brought to Kano at the time of the Crusades and has been kept there as ceremonial regalia ever since. The hundred tall, black horsemen, clad in the armour of the Middle Ages, black ostrich plumes waving in their helmets, their horses caparisoned in long coats almost down to their fetlocks, and with high-pommelled, richly decorated riding-saddles, came thundering at the aircraft and passengers, each warrior with his left hand on the reins, his right holding aloft a lance. They rode at full gallop till they were some 20 feet from the passengers; then suddenly each reined in his horse, each horse coming to a violent stop and sinking to its front knees, each warrior rising upright in his saddle with a shout, and a great cloud of dust billowing across them. The salute of medievalism to modernity.

Permission to refuel at Fort Lamy in French colonial territory, when French Equatorial Africa declared for the Free French, enabled this route to be reopened early in July 1940, from Takoradi on the Gold Coast to Cairo. The services of SABENA (the Belgian air line), who were still operating in the Belgian Congo although their homeland was in possession of the enemy, were also requested. It should be said at once that the Belgians in the Congo co-operated in this matter, as in all others, with the greatest willingness and friendliness. They first linked up their existing Congo service with the Horseshoe Section at Entebbe under charter to British Overseas Airways; and shortly they started a trans-African route to supplement our own, flying between Takoradi and Juba, and extending later at our request to Cairo. They had few aircraft and, since their home organisation was in enemy hands, fewer spare parts, but they kept their services flying with excellent regularity in such circumstances.

All these measures remained only palliatives. Official mail and freight, carried by sea from Britain to West Africa, could be flown swiftly to Cairo, but the hard fact persisted that there was no all-air communication between Britain and her Middle East Forces.

It happened that, while all this was going on, two ground officials of British Overseas Airways were making their way by car and river steamer across the heart of Africa, seeking the possibility of a flying-boat route along the river Congo. When Italy declared war there were three flying-boats needed on the Horseshoe Section which it was intended to fly out to Durban via West Africa and the Congo river, connecting with the main Empire route at Lake Victoria. A cable was therefore sent at once to Mr. Crudge, then the regional director in Central Africa, instructing him to make the journey from Nairobi to the mouth of the Congo, to survey possibilities. He started on June 13th, taking as assistant Mr. Scott-Hill, and had sent his preliminary report by July 7th, finding the route feasible, though no flying-boats had ever traversed it before and no ground-organisation existed.

Crudge returned to Nairobi, leaving Scott-Hill at Leopoldville, the capital of the Belgian Congo, to await events.

On the bank of the Congo immediately opposite to Leopoldville lies Brazzaville, the capital of French Equatorial Africa. At that time, of course, the Government of that colony had sided with Vichy France. The story now shifts back to England, where the two Empire S.30 flying-boats *Clare* and *Clyde* had just resumed the transatlantic flights of the 1940 series. On the evening of August 5th *Clyde* lay at her moorings in Poole harbour, prepared to start on the Atlantic run the following day. There were sudden telephone instructions for her captain, Captain A.C. Loraine, to depart next morning, not for America, but for Lagos, on the West Coast of Africa; he would be carrying a load of important passengers.

Only an expert could realise quite what that order entailed. Captain Loraine was faced with a journey of some 5,000 miles – the stretch between Lisbon and Bathurst is in itself about equal to an Atlantic crossing – over a route which had never before been flown by a flying-boat. Because of the war, he would not be able to alight in French colonial territory, but must hop from Poole to Lisbon, Lisbon to Bathurst in the Gambia (a flight of 1,900 miles), Bathurst to Freetown in Sierra Leone, and Freetown to Lagos in Nigeria (a flight of 1,400 miles). He would have no radio to help his navigation, and absolutely no weather reports at all once he had passed Lisbon. There would be no airways staff in West Africa to carry out the specialised task of refuelling a flying-boat (without sinking it), no proper equipment, no engineering facilities should anything go wrong.

His party of passengers arrived at Poole next morning and proved to be staff officers of General de Gaulle's newly formed Free French movement, headed by General de Larminat. With Captain W.S. May as second pilot, and Radio Officer Cheeseman as the only other member of the crew, Loraine took off in Clyde from Poole on August 6th, alighting a few hours later at Lisbon without incident. At nightfall the flarepath was laid across the harbour. *Clyde* started her run, her forward lights switched on to help in the take-off, for she was carrying a load of 53,000 lb. – greater than such an aircraft had ever before lifted.

May, sitting on the right-hand of his captain, looked out ahead while Loraine concentrated on lifting *Clyde* from the water. In his own words: "I saw what I took to be a thin searchlight, of the kind that we have for testing cloud-height, on the hills across the harbour ahead of us. Suddenly I realised that this 'searchlight' was on the water immediately in our path; that a small ship, probably a fishing vessel, lay directly in front of us, and what I saw was our own lights shining on a sail furled round her mast.

"I shouted to Loraine, but he was concentrating on take-off, and I was not sure whether he had heard me, for the ship was slightly to my side, placed so that he could not easily see it. Just then we became airborne, flying only a few feet above the water straight for the vessel. It seemed impossible to miss it. I shouted again."

At that moment both pilots acted simultaneously – May, in this emergency, acting as "I have never done before, and hope I shall never have to do again," – seizing the controls together and flinging *Clyde* hard to port. The starboard wing lifted just sufficiently to clear the ship's masthead; the port wing can have missed hitting the water by only a few inches. Then they were climbing in flight, and safe.

They flew all night. When dawn came they were flying south with that interminable coastline of western Africa on their left. That must be the longest, emptiest beach in the world; it runs for thousands of miles, never varying save where, occasionally, it is broken by the outlet to the sea of some lazy swampland. They flew hour after hour with always the same view – a thin yellow strip of beach, edged with white as the surf pounds it, with a hinterland of flat brown desert or brown-green swamp, great stretches of it without even a palm-tree to break the line.

May went below to speak to the passengers, and saw through the window a large V-shaped tear beneath the starboard wing, just beyond the outer motor, with a whole section of the aileron torn out. They had not missed the ship's mast. However, *Clyde* was flying well and they continued to Bathurst, alighting on the wide stretch of water at the mouth of the Gambia river nearly 15 hours after leaving Lisbon.

Bathurst, a fully equipped flying-boat base and perhaps destined to be one of the big air stations of the world on the Europe-South America routes, was then nothing but a bedraggled, miserable, hot and humid, forgotten little town built behind a small quay known as Half Die – grim reminder of the ravages of some previous tropical epidemic. In pre-war days, the German Lufthansa had built a small airfield eight miles up-river, and had left behind them a piece of aircraft metal which conveniently fitted the gap in *Clyde*'s aileron; some naval engineers obliged with a few heavy brass nuts and bolts with which to fix it.

They spent that night at Bathurst and continued next day to Freetown, some 450 miles farther round the coast. Freetown, though much larger and more prosperous than Bathurst – there is even a comic little railway running up-country into the bush-covered mountains behind the port – was equally unaccustomed to flying-boats. The problem here was to get some fuel into *Clyde*'s tanks. A flying-boat on the water is a fragile craft, easily damaged by a bump from a barge in a swiftly flowing current. To his horror, Loraine saw a steel barge of several hundred tons, carrying petrol in heavy drums, bearing down on her with the intention of refuelling her; his urgent signals persuaded the barge to keep clear.

Refuelling *Canopus* at Olvendo on the Congo. The local staff are using a dugout canoe and a modern launch; both are padded to protect the delicate skin of the flying-boat.

They tackled the problem again next day, in a quiet bay upstream where Loraine moored *Clyde* to an old buoy, and the drums of petrol were brought alongside in native canoes, hoisted on to the wings, and the fuel poured into the tanks through a funnel, under the protection of Loraine's raincoat which had to be held over the funnel all day to keep out the tropical rain which drenched down throughout the ceremony. By nightfall, having worked all day in tropical heat and rain, they had put 1,000 gallons of petrol into the tanks. It had to suffice. Next morning Clyde took off from Freetown, flew 1,300 miles, and alighted at the much bigger port of Lagos, where the damaged wing could be more efficiently repaired, although even here there were no engineering facilities for flying-boats. The natives referred to *Clyde* in pidgin English as "the canoe that goes for up."

Loraine had now accomplished the task which had been set him. He had brought his flying-boat over an untried route of 5,000 miles without any aid but his own skill, and had delivered his important passengers at Lagos. But more was yet to be asked of him, for the political situation in the French colonies had become difficult. The authorities in French Equatorial Africa adhered firmly to Vichy. The matter resolved itself into this – should we have to fight for those vast stretches of tropical Africa which were vital to our communications with the Middle East, or could the de Gaullists seize power and bring them over to our side without war? General de Larminat had been flown to Africa for that very purpose.

Some preliminary work had already been done. A little earlier our merchant aircraft from West Africa had flown two British officers from Lagos to Leopoldville, the Belgian city on the Congo immediately opposite the French capital of Brazzaville. These two officers had already started the game, crossing the river quietly by night, mixing with the pro-Allies Frenchmen in Brazzaville, and distributing leaflets, some of which even found their way on to the desk of the Vichy governor, General Husson, himself. It had been discovered that a number of officers and officials in Brazzaville were not particularly pro-Vichy, but they knew little of the de Gaullist movement, and had suspicions of it. It was necessary to secure their adhesion more firmly before any coup d'état could be attempted; it was urgently necessary, therefore, that General de Larminat should be flown on at once to the Congo, to meet these men and bring them over to the Allied side.

The problem was how to get him there, for the risks of landing to refuel in French territory with the de Gaullists on board were too great. The only aircraft available that could fly direct from Lagos to Leopoldville was *Clyde* herself, but the risks of attempting to put her down on the Congo river were also formidable. No flying-boat had ever alighted before on that broad stretch of the Congo that flows at great speed between Leopoldville and Brazzaville; nobody knew whether a flying-boat could find there an alighting area of sufficient size, free from snags beneath the surface. But it was decided in London to risk *Clyde* on the flight after all, so on August 19th she took off from Lagos and headed for Leopoldville.

Scott-Hill, the Airways man who had been left at that city after the ground survey of the Congo, marked out an alighting area on the river while *Clyde* was actually in flight; she was already overhead as he finished the job of anchoring safe moorings for her in the swift stream. Loraine brought her down safely on to the Congo, and de Larminat was taken ashore on the Belgian side.

Clyde had one more part to play in the drama. The most hopeful, from our point of view, of the French officers in Brazzaville was Colonel Carretier, commanding the French air force units there, a noted airman who had himself flown the South Atlantic. What more natural, then, than that

Scott-Hill should send him an invitation to cross the river to inspect the big British flying-boat which had just accomplished the remarkable feat of arriving on the Congo? Carretier came, and found de Larminat aboard. And there, in *Clyde*'s saloon, they worked out the details of the coup d'état which successfully surprised Brazzaville a few days later, and brought over to the Allies the great colony of French Equatorial Africa and its safe air route to the Middle East.

By that time *Clyde* was already on her way home. There were no facilities on the Congo to give her the engineering overhaul which she should have had after such a flight. The automatic pilot went wrong and Loraine and May had to take it in turns to fly her by hand over 3,500 miles of the route. When they returned safely to England, they had flown 12,000 miles where no flying-boat had ever been before, without ground services or navigational aids, the last part of the flight by hand. Loraine had done this in spite of a severe fever which had attacked him in Africa, and which put him straight into hospital on his return to England.

The primary purpose of *Clyde*'s great flight had been to bring French Equatorial Africa over to de Gaulle, and thus to avert what might have been a bitter war in the African jungles; it had been a complete success. But the flight had done something else of high importance also. It had re-established the link of air communications between besieged Britain and the Empire air routes. *Clyde* herself had to go back for the rest of the summer on to the transatlantic routes, so a regular service could not be started until the winter, although occasional flights were made. But by winter the route was brought into action from Britain to Lagos. Once that was accomplished, official despatches, and later mail for the troops as well, flew in a few days from inside the siege-walls of the British Isles to any part of the Allied or neutral world. Most important of all, official documents, passengers and urgent freight could pass between Britain and the Middle East Forces by an all-air route, on the flying-boat service between Britain and West Africa, and in the land-planes between West Africa and Cairo.

Before the regular route to West Africa was formally established there were three more flying-boat flights which not only confirmed its practicability, but extended it across the rivers of Central Africa to form a new link with the Horseshoe Section.

Three flying-boats left Britain at the end of September 1940, making for Lagos with a stop at Las Palmas in the Canary Islands. *Corinthian*, Captain J.C. Harrington, went first, followed at intervals of a few days by *Cassiopeia* and *Cooee*. From West Africa, Captain Harrington led the flight to Leopoldville, skirting the coastal area near Libreville where Vichy and Free French forces were disputing the last corners of the French colonies, and alighting on the Congo river as *Clyde* had done.

From there he followed the broad curves of the great river that hurries the mud half across Africa to spew it in a fawn-coloured semi-circle far into the South Atlantic. Once again this was a route which no flying-boat had ever before attempted, and on the ground were only a few Airways men who had hurried to the main halts to arrange that whatever decrepit launches were available should carry out refuelling; of ground engineering there was none.

He flew north-eastwards from Leopoldville over bush country, rapidly thickening into jungle, through which the brown Congo wound with many islands, arriving in the afternoon at Stanleyville. Mr. J.P. Ryan, an Airways man, had been sent down from Egypt to prepare for him, had laid moorings in the lee of a small island just below the town, had hung a windsock from a palm tree, and had engaged as control launch an elderly local motor-boat, "completely disguised with old tyres, sacking and bits of string" which could just make headway against the current provided the engine did not fail too frequently. He had been patrolling the area for two hours before Corinthian arrived, clearing away such oddments as floating tree-trunks; once she had alighted he worked at refuelling her from an improvised barge until nearly midnight, his only consolation being that, when he at last came wearily ashore, three naked little boys marched ceremoniously towards him and prostrated themselves in the mud – token, he thought, that somebody at least realised the importance of the Station Superintendent! As the other two flying-boats followed, Ryan had considerable trouble because of excitement among the local inhabitants. He could not prevent their setting off downstream in fleets of dugout canoes (fortunately on the wrong day) to welcome the "great birds'" whose arrival they anticipated.

Trouble of another kind awaited the third flying-boat Cooee when Captain F.J. Bailey brought her as far as Leopoldville. She lay moored in mid-river for the night, one officer left aboard her to keep watch. Late at night those ashore were summoned hastily to the river by a white Very signal. Through pelting rain they took the launch out to her, a journey of some 15 minutes, to find that a whole tree, 60 feet in length, washed into the river by the rains, lay fixed across Cooee's mooring rope. The two imminent dangers were either that the rope would snap and the flying-boat would be swept downstream in darkness, or that the tree would break loose and stove in her hull. The captain climbed aboard and started her engines, while the rest of the party tried to tug the tree clear with the launch, but at each attempt their gear parted. One man went ashore to fetch a steam tug, while the others laboured all through the night to save the flying-boat. Even the tug could not drag the tree clear. They toiled all night, and at dawn, in desperation, cut the mooring rope in the hope that the flying-boat, of lighter construction than the tree, would drift downstream the faster and have time to swing out of the way. The captain managed to get her clear just as the tree swept by.

In spite of incidents such as these, inseparable from an uncharted route through remote jungles, the three flying-boats all passed safely across the Congo, linked with the Horseshoe Section at Lake Victoria, and proceeded to Durban to join the main fleet.

In this way, not only was the main Empire route need-fully reinforced, but the pioneer work was done for another main route across Central Africa; to the old land-plane route through Kano to Khartoum there had now been added, farther to the south, a flying-boat route up the Congo river and down the Nile.

It was to come into operation in the early months of the following year, and prove invaluable in the task that was then to be laid upon the merchant air lines – that of carrying heavy burdens of war supplies across Central Africa to help nurture the fighting Forces of the Middle East.

PART III

THE BATTLE FOR AFRICA

'It's a Long Way'. The 'Horseshoe' passenger from Durban has curved half round the world. The last stage has brought him over the vast tracts of Northern Australia, down to the green coast of New South Wales. Now the signpost at Rose Bay, Sydney, points back through the global distance which, in peacetime, was the airway home.

CHAPTER 8

The Shadow Moves East

"VICTORY IS THE beautiful, bright-coloured flower," wrote Mr. Winston Churchill. "Transport is the stem without which it could never have blossomed. Yet even the military student, in his zeal to master the fascinating combinations of the actual conflict, often forgets the far more intricate complications of supply."

Throughout the war those complications have been the primary concern of the British Merchant Air Service. In the year 1941 the airmen were woven even more closely than before into the pattern of military supply; and as, in that year, while the British Isles were withstanding the German air assault, the Army played its main action on the stages of Africa and the Middle East, the air transport story also centred mainly in those regions.

It is necessary to recall briefly what happened in the Middle East war zone during 1941. At the opening of the year General Wavell's forces, few in number, overthrew and destroyed the Italian forces in the Libyan desert, simultaneously advancing to an even mightier, though somewhat more deferred defeat of those in East Africa and Abyssinia. Some of the desert troops were sent to join a few squadrons of the RAF who had already been strengthening the gallantry of the Greeks in defence of their country.

In spring and summer the weight of German force came to replace that of the enfeebled Italians in the Mediterranean theatre; the thinly stretched British were driven back across the desert to the Egyptian border, and compelled to remove altogether from Greece and Crete. The Germans planned for a far more ambitious drive to the east, based on an uprising of the Iraqi. The uprising duly took place, but the defence of Crete had so delayed German plans that they could not assist the rebels in time, and the scheme misfired. In logical counter-measure, the British advanced into Syria and removed its government from the men of Vichy. After a quieter autumn, during which remnants of Italian opposition were cleared away in Abyssinia, General Auchinleck's men moved forward across the Western Desert in a second successful campaign; while in the Far East, Japanese aggression began its assault towards Burma and Singapore.

In all these grave matters the merchant airmen had their share. At home they endured the German blitz in the same manner as everybody else, suffering considerable damage from German bombing, including the loss of Maia, the under-half of the famous composite flying-boat, which was sunk by enemy action in Poole harbour.

Overseas, they were first able to show their reactions to emergency in the evacuation of British troops from Crete. On April 22nd, 1941, the British Overseas Airways captain in charge at Cairo of the flying-boat operations was called hastily to the RAF Middle East headquarters and asked if he could organise immediately a ferry service to Crete, to evacuate British troops. There was no time to arm the flying-boats, and although fighter protection would be given if possible, it seemed highly unlikely to materialise. Luckily, he had a spare flying-boat in Cairo; he promised that the Crete ferry service should start that same day.

An hour and a half later Captain J.L.M. Davys was flying Coorong northwards from Cairo to Alexandria, where RAF ground staff began to spray her with camouflage paint. They had time to camouflage only the top of the wings by late afternoon, when Captain Davys took off again for Suda Bay, in Crete. He set off with his head full of emergency instructions, including orders to fly close to the water and to avoid the British fleet, which was shooting on sight – an instruction which a cruiser underlined by opening fire on him before he had been flying for an hour. Coorong was flying alone; there was no fighter escort. When she reached Crete she crept round the mountains to hide from various hostile aircraft dotted about the sky, and alighted in Suda Bay without incident, picking her way among sunken ships and tying up by a tanker. It was darkening, so the crew went ashore, but the only accommodation they could find was a stone barn among the olive groves containing a packing case, a blanket, a hurricane lamp, some dirty plates, and a few bottles of beer. Before dawn their passengers turned up – 35 men, unshaven and unwashed but cheerful enough, each clasping his tin hat and some small souvenir of Greece. Coorong took off when the mountain tops were just hardening in the first light, and flew safely to Alexandria.

By this time a second flying-boat, Cambria, had arrived with Captain F.V.W. Foy in command, to join the ferry. Foy and Davys flew back to Crete on this second afternoon of the evacuation, formating with an RAF Sunderland flying-boat with four comforting guns protruding from her tail. The crews slept on board their flying-boats in Suda Bay that night, and next morning both took off with two more loads of evacuees, most of them air crews of the RAF whose aircraft had been shot from beneath them.

So, throughout those painful days, the air ferry plied back and forth between the perils of Crete and the haven of Alexandria. The problem in Egypt was not only to supply the Crete ferry, but to do so without interrupting the normal running of the Horseshoe Section, carrying high priority war loads, from which the aircraft and crews had to be drawn. It was most ingeniously done.

As each flying-boat arrived on a normal Horseshoe service at Cairo, its

At Singapore, air and sea gateway to the East, the flying-boats turned again for Africa while Qantas air-crews continued the route south to Australia. Before the Japanese war, Empire flying-boats lay thick in Singapore.

crew was rushed in a fast car along the desert road to Alexandria, to take its turn on the Crete ferry; the same car brought back to Cairo the weary crew from the previous Crete ferry, who at once took over the Horseshoe aircraft and continued its flight to Durban or to Singapore. Coorong and Cambria, with a changing roster of crews in this manner, made 13 return trips to Crete between April 22nd and May 5th, and brought out a total of 469 British troops.

All normal standards were ignored. The method of loading the flying-boats was to allow the troops to file in until the forward door was so low that water began to pour in; then the door was slammed, and the flying-boat took off. On some trips more than 50 passengers were carried in an aircraft built for 21. The airmen were proud to have been allowed to lend a hand, and rightly pleased that they had done so without, in the tradition of the merchant service, any notable interruption of the normal air line schedules.

The next enemy sally cut across the Horseshoe Section itself. Some 60 miles west of Baghdad, on the shores of Lake Habbaniya in Iraq, there is a large, permanent RAF station which was being used as an engineering and flying-training base. Perched on the lake-shore a mile or two from this station was a rest-house belonging to British Overseas Airways, for Habbaniya had been a regular port of call ever since flying-boats were used on the Empire route to the Far East.

Towards the end of April 1941, forces of the Iraqi, under the usurped premiership of Rashid Ali, and at German instigation, gathered on the plateau above the RAF station and threatened it with a siege. The manner in which these forces were beaten off, largely by pupils of the RAF school in obsolete training aircraft, and in which a relief force from Palestine received the surrender of Baghdad, is now well known. A small battle, but its loss might well have cost us the whole of the Middle East.

Merchant airmen of India played a part in this battle. Three D.C.2 aircraft of Tata Airlines, one of the two big internal air lines of India, were put under the orders of the RAF in order to fly reinforcements and supplies from Karachi to Basra, in southern Iraq. Their pilots were called temporarily into the Air Force reserve – Flight Lieutenant L. Egglesfield, then Deputy Director of Civil Aviation for India, Flight Lieutenant B.W. Figgins, the air superintendent of Tata Airlines, and Pilot Officer A. Richardson, of Indian National Airways. Their second pilots, C.V. Gadgil, D.K. Jatar and K.R. Guzder, were all Indian airmen. As the battle of Habbaniya broke out, these men flew from Basra to Habbaniya itself, carrying ammunition in, and bringing women and children out, flying on many occasions through artillery and small-arms fire. Figgins, in addition, located and rescued the crew of an RAF bomber which had crashed in the desert.

Meanwhile the Horseshoe Section had been interrupted by the outbreak of hostilities, and the Airways men stationed at Habbaniya and Baghdad had been cut off by the enemy.

By April 31st Mr. Thomson, in charge of the rest-house at Habbaniya, had evacuated, on two flying-boats which passed through, all the women and children; the only Europeans remaining at the rest-house were six men of Airways ground staff. They were, of course, entirely unarmed. They watched the Iraqi troops digging in on the plateau, and saw the battle open, prospects which caused their own locally engaged staff to slide gently away into the desert.

On the evening of May 3rd, the Airways rest-house was surrounded by a party of Arabs, who behaved with reasonable friendliness. But next evening these were reinforced by some Iraqi soldiers, who ordered the Airways men from the house, stripped them of their valuables, shackled their wrists and drove them away in a lorry to the neighbouring town of Falluja, a journey during which they were twice bombed and machine-

Habbaniya Rest-House, oasis in the long flight across the Syrian desert. It was near here that the resistance of a small RAF training school frustrated Rashid Ali and helped to save the Middle East. The rest-house was looted by Iraqi rebels.

gunned by RAF aircraft. In the early hours of the following morning they were driven in another lorry to Baghdad, where they were housed at last in a concentration camp with some other civilians of British nationality who had been captured. There they remained until June 1st, when the Iraq rebellion had been beaten down.

Baghdad was still in an uproar. The Iraq rebel army, or what remained of it, had come into the town fully armed and was leading an outbreak of mob violence. One Airways man, driving to his office that evening, was fired upon by a lorry load of Iraqi. All that night the town was full of small-arms fire, and several hundred Jews were massacred. Not until June 3rd was quiet restored, so that the Airways men could get permission to return to their rest-house at Habbaniya. They found that it had been completely gutted; nevertheless, two of them from the concentration camp went straight back to work in the ruins, and organised ground service for the flying-boat route.

Fortunately, the C-class flying-boats were in the process of being fitted with extra tanks, giving them longer range. Those that had been thus adapted were put on to a shuttle service between Cairo and Bahrain, overflying Iraq altogether, and thus linking up the two ends of the Horseshoe. For a time a refuelling halt was established at Akaba, where the southernmost tip of Palestine touches the northern waters of the Red Sea, a motor yacht, Imperia, being stationed there as depot ship. It was necessary to swing the route thus to the south while fighting was proceeding in Iraq, and later when the British moved into Syria, for the anticipation was of a German assault southwards, aimed at the Suez Canal. When no such assault materialised, it became possible to return to the flying-boat station at Tiberias on the Sea of Galilee; but a more southerly station was preferable, and it was eventually selected at Kallia, on the Dead Sea, close to the ruins of Jericho, through which the flying-boats went on to be normally routed.

CHAPTER 9

The Trans-African Lifelines

IT WILL BE seen that both the evacuation ferry from Crete, and the troubles in Iraq, were only incidentals in the story of military supply by the merchant airmen in the Middle East campaigns of 1941. They had two main tasks – to maintain the air communications between London and Cairo for urgent despatches and supplies, and to operate a local air transport system behind the armies engaged in the fighting zones.

In the earlier part of the year the only possible all-air route from Britain to Egypt lay via the West Coast of Africa. It fell into two parts, which were separately organised – that from Britain to Nigeria, known as the "West African route"; and that from Nigeria, across Africa to Cairo, known as the "Trans-African route."

The West African route, pioneered by Captain Loraine in *Clyde*, could be managed at that time only by flying-boats. *Clare* and *Clyde* had been put on to regular West African service in October 1940, and continued to fly it in the following year. On the night of February 14th-15th *Clyde* lay at her moorings at Lisbon, with only a Portuguese workman on board her.

A hurricane, said to be the worst that Portugal had experienced for 87 years, sprang up quite unannounced, spreading destruction through the city; the damage was estimated at £10,000,000. Buildings were struck down, the beach between Lisbon and Estoril was pounded by great waves for that night and the whole of the following day, gusts of wind were recorded exceeding a speed of 100 miles an hour. When the storm broke, the crew of *Clyde* hurried to the shore to find her gallantly riding out the wind and seas at her own anchor, the waves breaking right over her. The airmen tried to put out to her in a boat, but after several attempts had to desist; all they could do was to stand and watch *Clyde* fighting the hurricane on her own. She rode it for hours, proving her seaworthiness, and the men ashore began to hope that she might survive. Then a piece of floating wreckage was hurled against her port wing, puncturing the float; at almost the same moment an extremely fierce gust lifted her starboard wing and she turned turtle. The Portuguese workman was drowned. *Clyde* was a total loss, for when they got her ashore at Cabo Ruivo she was nothing but a hulk.

That left only *Clare* on the West African section of the vital air link to the Middle East; it was urgent to supplement her, and to her aid came an aircraft with one of the most unusual histories of the air behind her. In 1939 Mr. Richard Archbold made an expedition to New Guinea to study birds,

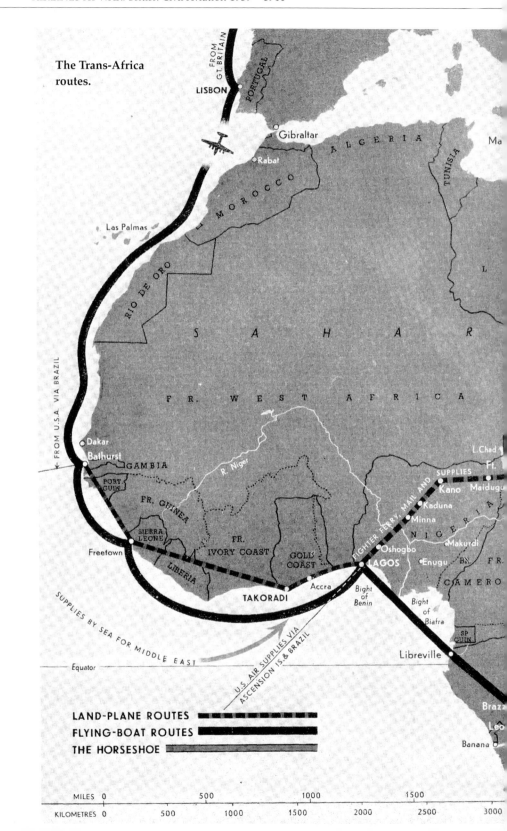

The Trans-Africa routes.

LAND-PLANE ROUTES
FLYING-BOAT ROUTES
THE HORSESHOE

MILES 0   500   1000   1500
KILOMETRES 0   500   1000   1500   2000   2500   3000

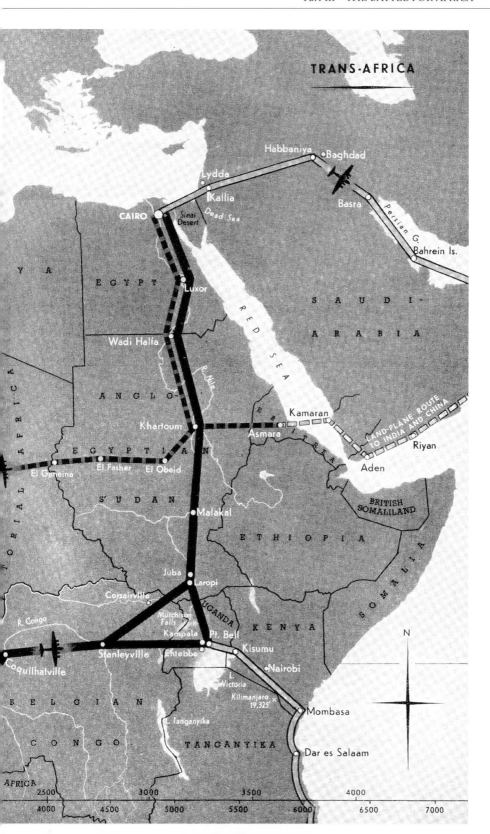

TRANS-AFRICA

mammals and plants for the American Museum of Natural History. He used for his expedition a version of the United States naval PBY flying-boat, of a type which is became familiar to the RAF as the Catalina.

This aircraft was named *Guba*. After her successful expedition to New Guinea, the Australian Government commissioned her, in 1939, to make a survey flight across the Indian Ocean to Mombasa, in Kenya. Then she crossed Africa to Dakar, and proceeded across the Atlantic via the Virgin Islands, to appear at the New York World's Fair before traversing America to San Diego, California. The British Air Commission purchased her in 1940, and in October of that year, piloted by Captain I.G. Ross, a Canadian pilot of British Overseas Airways, she flew the North Atlantic from Newfoundland to Scotland, without oxygen or heating in a temperature well below freezing point. She was the first bomber purchased in wartime from America to be delivered to Britain across the North Atlantic. When she arrived, however, she was, at Lord Beaverbrook's suggestion, prepared for transport, handed to British Overseas Airways, and placed alongside Clare on the West African route in March 1941.

In the next few months the West African fleet was still further increased. Two more Empire flying-boats were added, and later another Catalina, converted from the military type. Still the load that could be carried was insufficient for the urgency of communications with Cairo, and the hard-pressed aircraft industry of Britain had all it could do to meet the demands for fighting aircraft. Britain therefore purchased from Pan-American Airways three large Boeing flying-boats – the Clippers of the American merchant air service – which we named Bristol, Berwick and Bangor. They were purchased primarily for the West African route, but facilities for their maintenance did not exist in Britain. British Overseas Airways therefore set up a maintenance base at Baltimore, U.S.A., to which the Boeings returned for servicing after each round flight between Britain and West Africa. In this way a transatlantic service developed.

While the section of the air route from Britain to West Africa was thus maintained and strengthened, that second section, from West Africa to Egypt, was also much increased. The airmen were continually pressed to this task for three main reasons – the RAF had established an engineering base at Takoradi on the Gold Coast for assembling fighters brought by sea and flying them on to the Middle East Forces, and a merchant service was needed to bring back the ferry pilots for fresh loads; vital equipment supplied for the Middle East Forces from America under lease-lend arrangements was accumulating in the West African ports and needed to be hastened across Africa to the battle; and to the official mail and despatches which were carried to and from Cairo by the all-air route were now added troop mail across Africa, and special light-weight post card mail over the whole route. To the original, somewhat motley land-plane fleet which had been plying trans-Africa were added, in the last days of 1940. a number of D.H.86 aircraft brought back from the Far East.

A small fleet of the new K-class (Flamingo) aircraft was also being assembled in Britain for transfer to the trans-Africa route, though they were to prove sadly disappointing in actual operation under tropical conditions, and had eventually to be grounded. Lockheed Lodestars were being shipped into Cape Town from America to join with the Lockheed 14s already in Africa and form an L-class fleet, destined to replace all other aircraft on the internal African services of British Overseas Airways, supplemented afterwards by the big E-class (Ensign) aircraft. SABENA, the Belgian air line already operating trans-Africa under charter to British Overseas Airways, continued its services to supplement the route. But all was still insufficient to shift the heavy priority loads accumulating in West Africa, and to bring back from Cairo the ever-increasing number of RAF ferry pilots on what had become the aerial life-line of the Middle East Forces.

The stalwart Empire flying-boats were therefore called in to help. The route along the Congo river which had been pioneered by *Corinthian*, *Cassiopeia* and *Cooee* on their way to Durban the previous September, was opened up into a regular service, a second great trans-African route matching the land-plane route farther north.

At Lagos, the western terminus, Airways ground staff toiled through tropical heat to provide the necessary facilities; others arrived all along the line to open up intermediate stations. Moorings were laid, launches and adequate refuelling barges were gradually acquired – though there were still occasions when passengers were disembarked from that most modern craft, the flying-boat, into that most ancient craft, the native canoe hollowed from a tree-trunk. The natives grew accustomed to the sight of the "canoes that go for up" dropping down from the skies, or taking off from lagoons and river-stretches with a roar and widening white wake. But they never really reconciled themselves to the necessities of air travel.

Considerably later, when a more suitable alighting area was chosen at Lagos, it happened to be in a lagoon which native fishermen were wont to use at night. Nothing could persuade them that there was any danger in unlit fishing canoes wandering about a lagoon on which flying-boats were alighting; one delighted fisherman, indeed, was discovered with his canoe tied to one of the alighting flares, finding the lights served admirably to attract the fish. When the fishermen realised that they were really to be forbidden their night waters they grew angry, and employed a witch-doctor to put a ju-ju on the lagoon. This would not have mattered, except that the native employees of British Overseas Airways then refused to go near the place, until the corporation employed another witch-doctor to "de-ju-ju" it. (The Airways witch-doctor did not seem to be particularly powerful, since the Airways depot ship caught fire on the lagoon a few nights later, though that may be laid to the blame, perhaps, not of witchcraft but of a watchman who decided to refuel a petrol engine by the light of a hurricane lamp.)

These difficulties are not, after all, surprising. It is less than a century since H.M.S. *Bloodhound* and *Teazer* sent landing parties ashore to spike the guns of the native king of Lagos, in stockades of coconut trees where the biggest shops of the city faced the main street.

Lagos itself, for all its pleasant villas, well-kept streets, motor-cars, is but a thin European structure built on solid paganism. There is an atmosphere of attractive simplicity in the local in his smart, pearl-grey European suit, strolling down the main street with a pair of shoes balanced on his head; in the vivid colours of the women's clothing; in the eagerness with which the Nigerians undertake work that brings them into contact with the mechanics of civilisation. One Airways launch, for example, was placed in charge of a native coxswain with an unpronounceable name who was dubbed "Crew Apple." A most diligent and worthy coxswain he proved, his launch always the smartest of all, until it was decided to give him an assistant, a smaller African, of a name equally unpronounceable who was dubbed "Crew Banana." Then there was trouble, for Crew Apple was senior, prestige was at stake. Not until he was promoted and given a cap as badge of proud authority did the launch function properly again. It chugged up and down, once more the smartest on the lagoon, manned by Captain Apple (with cap) and Crew Banana.

From this terminus of Lagos the flying-boats carried the new Congo route south and west; south over the Bight of Benin ("Beware, beware, the Bight of Benin, Where few come out, though many go in"), into the Bight of Biafra on the Gulf of Guinea, to alight on the broad mouth of the Gabon river in the French Cameroons. There, in a thatched hut by the shore, shaded by palm trees, quite by herself lived a Dutchwoman of advancing years, choosing to inhabit this remote place because she preferred it to anywhere else in the world. From the first she welcomed the flying-boat crews and passengers, opening her hut to them, providing them with beer and lemonade, stocking a few cigarettes for them during the short hour of their refuelling halt, and in time becoming famous over all the air routes of the world.

Thence the flying-boats flew still farther down the coast, turning westwards at last into Africa, over jungle so dense that it seemed from above like a carpet of green moss, from which thin wisps of vapour steamed slowly upwards to the drifting white clouds; and thus on to the broad stretch of the racing Congo river at Leopoldville, where Belgians placed a large houseboat at the disposal of British Overseas Airways, and charged them for it a rental of one franc a year.

They spent the night at Leopoldville, taking off at dawn to follow the wide, deserted sweeps of the Congo river, the jungle thickening once more on either bank into impenetrability, up to the hamlet of Coquilhatville, almost plumb on the equator, where at the arrival of each flying-boat the river bank was always lined, football-grandstand fashion, by the entire local population, looking on in amazement but complete silence. The next hop, quite short, brought the flying-boats to Stanleyville, a pleasant township set in palm thickets and wattle villages, the pirogues of the chanting fishermen moving rapidly downstream below Stanley Falls, in silhouette against the sunset. Two other women made themselves famous over the air routes of Africa at Stanleyville. Mmes. Delva and Piedboeuf determined, immediately the flying-boat route opened, to form a small committee to entertain every airman and every soldier who passed through their town, meeting them at the riverside with cars, driving them round to see all the local sights, taking them for bathes, or possibly arranging canoe trips for them over the rapids at the Stanley Falls. By the end of 1943 these two ladies had thus entertained more than 6,000 men of the Services of the Allied nations.

It is not too far to fly from Stanleyville on to the regular Horseshoe route the following day, though the flying-boats passed over the remotest, most fabulous jungles of Central Africa – first the thick jungle of the pygmy territory, then the Mountains of the Moon. They had a glimpse or two of Lake Albert to the south, before alighting on the White Nile at Laropi, beneath the tall Nyeri mountains. The next stop was either Juba or Malakal on the White Nile, both stations on the old-established trunk air route of Africa; an easy journey thence to Khartoum and Cairo.

By full summer of 1941, therefore, there were two main trans-African routes, the land-planes to the north through Nigeria, the flying-boats to the south over the Congo. Still it was not enough. So, Britain gratefully accepted the offer of the United States Government, not then at war, to strengthen the trans-African routes, and to assist in the air transport of war materials, many of them lend-lease goods, to the Middle East where they were so badly needed. The United States Government contracted with Pan-American Airways for that company to open an air-transport service with flying-boats from New York, via Brazil and across the South Atlantic to the west coast of Africa; and onwards, with land-planes, from Bathurst in the Gambia to Khartoum. The land-planes used the regular trans-Africa route, and it was Britain's part to continue to provide the necessary facilities.

It was hoped that the American air line would provide such good capacity on this service that our own land-plane services could be taken off the route, for use as war transport elsewhere in Africa. Pan-American Airways (Africa) Ltd. brought in their men and aircraft with a will, starting regular flights at the end of October, and taking over the whole route as far as Khartoum before the end of the year. Our flying-boats continued to fly the Congo route, but our land-planes were all concentrated on the section of the route between Khartoum and Cairo, to carry on the loads which the Americans brought thus far. The arrangement was satisfactory for the moment.

Meanwhile the war situation in the Mediterranean area generally seemed to have improved considerably, and it was debated whether or not the air routes between Britain and Egypt could be swung back, at least in part, directly over the Mediterranean itself. The time that would be saved in avoiding the long detour through West Africa would, of course, be considerable. To be weighed against this was the risk involved. It meant flying unarmed, comparatively slow flying-boats directly across the enemy's own lines of communication; for the Germans were then on both sides of the Mediterranean air route, in Cyrenaica (the eastern coastal region of Libya) and Crete, and the Italians and Germans alike were beginning to work up to the determined assault on Malta from Sicily and Pantelleria.

It was decided to make the attempt, and to divert five flying-boats to this route from the West African. They were to fly from Britain via Foynes in Eire, Lisbon, Gibraltar, Malta, and Aboukir to Cairo.

Captain W.S. May took off in *Clare* on October 12th, leaving Foynes at midnight for Lisbon and spending the whole of that day there – the route was conditioned by weather forecasts for alighting in the tricky harbours at Gibraltar and Malta. They arrived at Gibraltar on October 14th, taking off again in the twilight for Malta, where they had to fly around for an hour waiting for dawn and permission to alight. Although the heavy assault on that island had not then begun, and only few enemy aircraft were crossing the coast, the warning sirens were already sounding an average of six times a day. At last light *Clare* took off for Cairo, flying roughly midway between Crete and the Libyan coast, from both of which enemy night-fighters were operating, and had recently shot down several of our aircraft. On this occasion the weather proved *Clare*'s worst enemy – she was boxed in with thunderstorms – but she managed to fly under the worst of it, and to reach Cairo in safety.

Three days later *Clare* made the return trip successfully, after a couple of nasty hours at Gibraltar. Not until they were almost on top of the Rock, doubly shrouded in complete darkness and thick cloud, was May able to determine his exact position. He radioed to Gibraltar to illuminate searchlights directly upwards from the Rock; when a faint reflection of the lights appeared on the cloud-tops, he spiralled down beside them, broke cloud at last and alighted. Among his passengers were some very senior officers who had an appointment (and kept it) that evening with the Prime Minister at 10 Downing Street.

Now this return flight by *Clare* was a notable achievement. It proved that the merchant air service could fly the vital link between Britain and the Middle East straight through the enemy's heavily armed battle lines. The five flying-boats continued to fly the "direct Mediterranean" with fair regularity through ever-increasing perils until the German advance across the Western Desert the following summer made it impossible.

CHAPTER 10

The Tedder Plan

ALL THE AFRICAN endeavours which have thus far been described were concerned with that one great problem, the supply line through the air from Britain to the Middle East. Behind the immediate battlefront inside Africa there was another problem of air communications and supply, in which the merchant airmen were equally engaged.

In June 1941 Air (Chief) Marshal Tedder, then recently appointed Air Officer Commanding-in-Chief, Middle East, stating that there was military need for increased air transport in Africa, to Palestine, Syria, Turkey and Iraq, and in the task of taking ferry pilots back over the African routes to bring up more reinforcement aircraft, suggested that a joint RAF-British Overseas Airways organisation should be formed to take over this commitment, with new transport aircraft that were expected from America; the whole thing to be under the direction of British Overseas Airways, with their long knowledge of air line operation. All this was to be in addition to the routes they were already flying in Africa.

Upon this signal was built a system of air communications internally in the Middle East area which came to be known as the "Tedder Plan." The system never became as comprehensive as the Air Marshal had envisaged, mainly owing to the dearth of technical staff and to the acute lack of spare parts for engines.

Nevertheless, it was, in the first place, a notable experiment in the proper application of air transport to the supply lines immediately behind the battle, under conditions of modern war; and in the event it proved something more than an experiment, for an air network was established to the military value of which the senior officers of the Middle East paid acknowledgment. "Were your services to be withdrawn," stated one letter from RAF headquarters, "communications would very quickly break down, with the most serious consequences to our military position in the Middle East."

Air Marshal Tedder felt, in brief, that it was more economical for the transport aircraft available to him to be organised on regular services by air line operators of experience, than for them to be dispersed among a number of transport squadrons allotted tasks as they came along.

At the same time it was an essential part of the Tedder Plan that all the transport aircraft could be gathered together, at periods of military

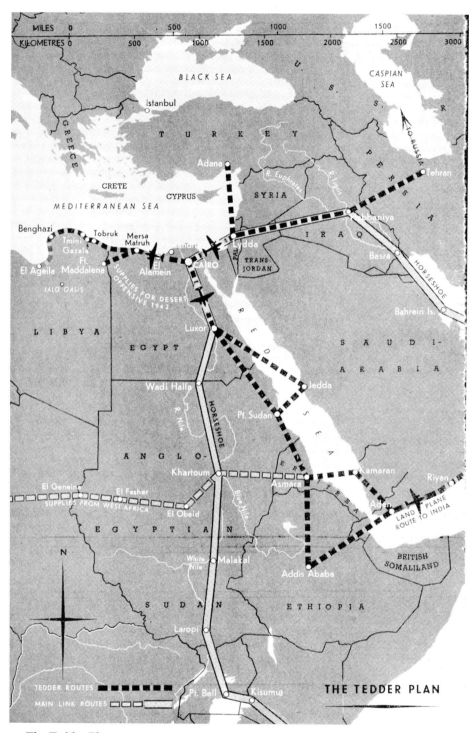

The Tedder Plan routes.

emergency, for the rapid movement of operational squadrons, personnel and supplies from one theatre of war to another, or for the carrying of urgent supplies to a battlefront.

The organisation of the Tedder Plan on the air line side fell to Mr. R.H. Maxwell, the Near East regional director of British Overseas Airways. One of his most pressing tasks was to set up an engineering base upon which the whole system of routes could be founded. It cannot be too firmly emphasised that air line operations of any kind depend fundamentally on the engineers; in this case, the amount of flying that could be done depended on the number of overhauled aircraft engines that could be produced on a regular programme, and that, in its turn, depended largely on the supply of spare parts from America, and the amount of skilled engineering labour which could be recruited. In peacetime these problems would not have seemed severe, but in wartime Middle East, spare parts were untold treasure, and a skilled engineer a bag of rubies.

Air Chief Marshal Sir Arthur Tedder, a portrait painted in May 1942. (Historic Military Press)

It was decided to place the engineering base sufficiently far from the battle to be reasonably assured against interruption from the enemy. The site chosen was Asmara, capital of the colony of Eritrea, which had been taken from the Italians. Raised on a verdant high plateau, surrounded for hundreds of miles by desert, this most attractive city in the European style stands in a country of perpetual springtime. The sun always shines by day; yet its heat is tempered by the altitude; the nights are always crisp. The countryside was strewn with dumps of scattered metal and mechanical equipment, there was excellent machinery in a big Fiat workshop in the town, and there was a number of skilled Italian mechanics only too eager to find employment.

The base was set up on the large airfield just outside the town. It had been heavily bombed during the British advance, and its buildings had to be reconstructed, mostly from scrap metal picked up around the place. The administrative buildings were all raised from Italian prefabricated huts of standard design, of which there were large stores nearby. The countryside was raked for pieces of machinery, and plenty were found, some of them sabotaged but few beyond quick repair. Dumps of crashed Italian aircraft were turned over for salvaged metal from which aircraft spares could be manufactured on the spot. So efficiently was scrap material they found in the country used, that a large engineering base was established at astonishingly small cost.

'Behind the Battle'. Refuelling a Lodestar transport at Asmara, Eritrea. At this large engineering base all the aircraft on the Tedder routes, which radiated the Middle East during the Libyan campaign, were serviced and kept airborne.

The staff which was formed in Asmara grew into a fully international unit. Its nucleus was a small number of British Airways engineers, but added to them were men of a dozen or more nations. Roughly 300 of them were Italians, who proved to be excellent workmen and gave practically no trouble, though they did grow a little cock-a-hoop when the German armies seemed to be doing rather better than usual. As time went on, British Overseas Airways cast the net of recruitment more widely. Palestinian Jews were brought into Asmara in some numbers, and with them refugees from Occupied Europe, many of them Poles and Czechs. They worked together harmoniously, although they could not produce the output which an all-British unit of the same size would have provided, and the flying hours of the Tedder Plan routes suffered accordingly.

The basic network of routes under the Tedder Plan was established during 1941. It radiated from Cairo, and its purpose was purely military; that is, the services were flown to carry military and Government personnel, and to give rapid communications for official mail. Two of the routes led southwards from Cairo, in order to carry RAF ferry pilots back to the aircraft pools, and to bring forward dumps of war supplies; one was the former trans-African route to the West Coast, the other led to Port Sudan. Two other routes led northwards from Cairo, to Tehran, the capital

An Armstrong Whitworth AW.27 Ensign, registration G-AFZU, pictured at Asmara, Eritrea, in 1942. (Historic Military Press)

of Persia and the supply gateway to Russia; and to Adana, in Turkey.

From the very start of the war Britain had wished to run a service into Turkey for diplomatic reasons, and the Turkish Government had not been averse. But she had been painfully short of the necessary aircraft; and the neutral Turks, who in 1940 had forbidden the German Lufthansa to enter their country on a plea of breach of hospitality, felt that they could not

A Lockheed Lodestar, registration G-AGBS, pictured at pictured at Asmara, Eritrea, in 1942. (Historic Military Press)

well sanction a British air service without reopening their airports to the Germans also. By full summer of 1941 the Turks had yielded so far as to allow the Germans to fly to Istanbul. Britain seized the opportunity and on September 3rd began a regular service between Cairo and Adana.

The Persian service had to await the end of the joint Anglo-Russian advance into that country which followed the Iraq rebellion. British Overseas Airways then carried out a survey of the route onwards from Habbaniya, over deep and spectacular mountain passes to Tehran, that delightful city, the broad streets of which gaze ever on a prospect of snow--capped peaks, and where there is always the sound of mountain streams racing along conduits to bubble into fountain pools set in the square green lawns of private gardens. The airfield facilities at Tehran were found to be much better than had been expected, and the regular service from Cairo began in November. It grew ever more important as Tehran became the great junction of the supply route for Allied aid to Russia, which was developed up the Persian Gulf, and across country to the capital.

Before leaving this Tedder Plan network, something should be said of two ancillary services, outside the plan itself but dovetailing with it. Misr Airwork, the Egyptian air line, carrying on gamely in conditions of difficulty owing to the lack of engineering spares, continued to be of great value to British air communications by providing a link between Egypt and the countries on the eastern shore of the Mediterranean. And far to the south, the Southern Rhodesia Air Services, incorporated in the Air Force at the outbreak of war, maintained a splendid network of communications throughout Southern Rhodesia which linked with the main Empire trunk routes on the Horseshoe Section. The merchant airmen of South Africa had gone, aircraft and all, into the South African Air Force, and their splendid war story lies in that of military operations.

In late autumn the air crews were given the chance, and gladly they took it, to put into action the other aspect of the Tedder Plan, carrying supplies to the battlefront. Throughout the summer the Middle East Forces had been accumulating a mass of supplies in Egypt, many of them brought over the air routes, in order to launch General Auchinleck's heavy assault against the Germans under Rommel in the Western Desert. A few days before the advance was due to start, the men of British Overseas Airways were called upon to fly a daily service between Cairo and the front, using Lodestar aircraft. One machine a day was called for at first, but before long this had been increased to three on regular service, and often five at times of crisis; for a while a night-mail service was flown from the battle area, reaching Cairo at dawn.

They carried many sorts of cargo. They always took both official and troops' mail, and senior officers of all Services who had either to hurry

'Nile Bird'. The white 'planes of the Misr Airlines, based on Cairo and flown by Egyptian pilots, played their own part in the supply battle which maintained the campaigns of the Middle East. They still fly in close co-operation with BOAC services.

forward into the battle area, or hasten back for a conference at Cairo head-quarters. On several occasions they carried the British commanders – General Auchinleck, Air Marshal Tedder, and General Freyberg. Their main westbound cargo was ammunition and light bombs, which they ferried to the forward fighter-squadrons; as the advance proceeded across Libya at a rapid pace, sometimes out-distancing the supply columns, the airmen rushed up hundreds of gallons of petrol in time, without which our fighter patrols would have been grounded.

For a brief period they carried water to our foremost troops, since the Germans had polluted the desert wells as they retreated. On the return journeys they ferried wounded men to hospital, and frequently they carried to captivity senior German and Italian officers who had been made prisoners. Throughout this campaign the merchant airmen lived in the desert amidst the same hardships as anybody else. They flew their aircraft through skies open to enemy fighters, just as the RAF did; the difference being that the merchant aircraft carried no guns. A few of them were fired at and hit in the air, fortunately without serious result, and one aircraft was badly damaged by enemy air attack as she stood on the ground.

Captains C.W.N.C. Pelly and V.A.M. Hunt were the first two captains to be employed on the Western Desert run, but before the campaign was over most of the air captains flying the internal African routes had taken their turn in the desert. Ground engineers queued up for the chance of being sent forward to tend the aircraft at the advanced desert landing grounds.

The first flights were to Maaten Bagush, the underground headquarters of the Desert Air Force, on the Egyptian coast near Mersa Matruh; and sometimes onwards about 140 miles to L.G.75, then the advanced fighter landing ground; or down south to the landing grounds around Fort Maddalena, on the frontier wire between Egypt and Libya, where the fighter squadrons waited to deploy into Cyrenaica. Much of the flying was done through dust-storms and rainstorms of the desert – at that time of the year there is no burning heat, but stormy weather and often intense cold. Sometimes it was easy to overshoot the big desert landing grounds, which were nothing but stretches of desert, similar to their surroundings, but scraped a little flatter. On one such occasion the captain, observing Fort Maddalena itself below him, inquired of an Air Force passenger whether it was "ours or theirs." "It was theirs yesterday," was the answer. "I don't know what happened to-day, but carry on for a few minutes and we'll soon know."

On the first day of the British assault, Captain Pelly was despatched from Cairo with sealed orders. They led him to the frontier area, where he picked up General Freyberg, to take him onward, over enemy-held desert, to Jalo, to get into contact with a formation of his New Zealand division, who were heavily engaged. Before the advance was many days old Captain Hunt left Cairo with two anonymous passengers, who proved to be General Auchinleck and Air Marshal Tedder on their way to Battle H.Q. in the desert. Next day he flew the Air Marshal to the most forward fighter-airfields, across which lay palls of dust as the squadrons took off for, and landed from their battle patrols. These were special flights, but the daily service continued without a break, following the advancing troops across the desert, with the western terminus rarely more than 20 miles behind the forward positions.

The flying in the forward areas all had to be done at only a few feet from the ground, to minimise the risk of enemy fighter interception, and of enemy anti-aircraft fire when the route led over one or other of the strongly held pockets behind the main advance. Few pilots went on the Western Desert run without finding themselves, at some time or another, sharing the sky with enemy fighters, or crouching behind the nearest stone while enemy strafers raked the landing-ground.

By mid-December the western terminal of the desert run had moved on to Bu Amud, near Tobruk. It was from there that they started the night-mail back to Cairo, in order that important despatches might be available to Middle East headquarters first thing in the morning, and that the troops'

A number of British merchant aircraft pictured at Almaya, Cairo, in 1944. Amongst the types is an Armstrong Whitworth Ensign. (Historic Military Press)

mail, that important item in any campaign, might get started on its homeward journey with the greatest possible speed.

On December 22nd there was a small crisis. The head of the advance had outstripped the supply columns, toiling along the dusty coast-road of the desert, and some of our Hurricanes were grounded for lack of fuel. Every merchant aircraft that could be immediately flown was collected at Heliopolis. Each managed to take aboard some 600 gallons of petrol, in tins. One was put out of action at an intermediate landing ground by running across a bomb-crater filled with soft sand, buckling its wing and undercarriage; the rest pushed on to the forward squadrons. Thus was the crisis overcome.

By then the daily service was running to Tmimi, a small village in Libya about fifty miles east of Derna and eighty miles west of Tobruk on the borders of the Djebel Akdar, the green country of Cyrenaica, and the merchant airmen were planning to extend to Benghazi. But they never reached that city. Rommel had turned at El Ageila, and the Eighth Army was being forced into its stubborn retreat as far as Gazala. The airmen continued their work throughout that short retreat, taking up supplies that were still more urgently needed, particularly ammunition. They still continued to bring back the important German and Italian prisoners, and one of the most precious cargoes they carried was a captured German cipher machine. Captain Pelly had been instructed to hand this over to nobody unless proper documents of authorisation were produced. When he reached Heliopolis airfield he hired a decrepit taxi in which he set off for Middle East headquarters in the centre of Cairo, clutching a rifle, to deliver his charge.

The Western Desert episode was nearly over. The airmen continued to fly for a few days more through dust-storms and rainclouds, taking supplies from one desolate stretch of sand and rock to another, flying sometimes over tank battles, sometimes through enemy fighter patrols. By the time the British line had been established at Gazala, the ordinary supply methods could cope with the demands, and the airmen went back, somewhat reluctantly, to the air routes that radiated from Cairo.

PART IV

JAPAN CUTS THE ROUTE

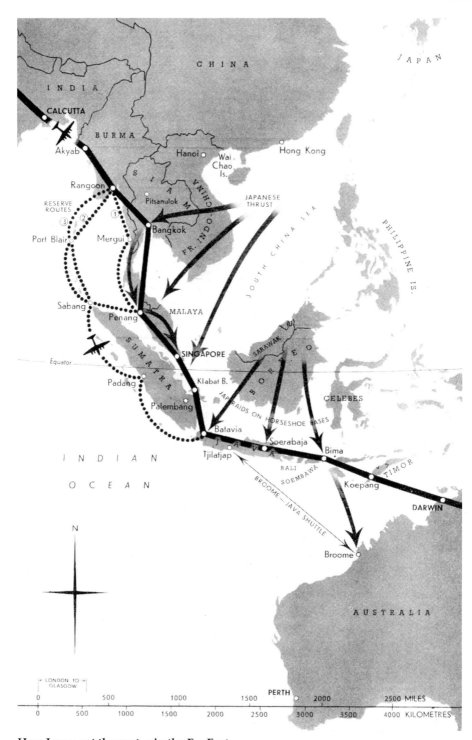

How Japan cut the routes in the Far East.

CHAPTER 11

Retreat from Malaya

LIKE SOME BROAD river flowing steadily, little heeding floods or drought that swell or empty lesser streams, the main Horseshoe Section of the Empire routes had been maintained regularly by the flying-boats plying back and forth between Durban and Sydney during the troubled year of 1941 in Africa. But now the main river itself was to be diverted, choked and dammed.

At the end of 1941 the Japanese stormed into the war in Asia and the Pacific.

Our air routes in the Far East had been hindered by the Japanese even before they came into the war. Japanese fighters, as has been described, shot up the aircraft Dardanus off the island of Wai Chao in 1939. In September of the following year the Japanese forced the French colonial authorities of Indo-China into an accommodation, and regular operations between Hong Kong and Bangkok – a branch from the Horseshoe Section – became an impossibility. The aircraft were removed to Africa, to supplement the fleet on the trans-Africa route. The air route to Hong Kong was suspended.

The main Horseshoe Section was still untouched. Having travelled from Durban, through Cairo, Palestine and Iraq, down the Persian Gulf to Karachi, and thence across northern India to Calcutta, the flying-boats of British Overseas Airways turned to the south across the Bay of Bengal to Rangoon in Burma, to Bangkok in Siam, and to Singapore; there the crews of Qantas Empire Airways, the Australian air line company, carried the aircraft onwards through the East Indies to Darwin in Australia, and round the north of that country to complete the journey in the harbour at Sydney. From Sydney the crews of Tasman Empire Airways flew on to Auckland, in New Zealand, making a connection with the trans-Pacific service of Pan-American Airways.

The vulnerability of this vital air route to Japanese aggression had been realised, and plans made to guard against it. Siam seemed to be the weakest link, with Burma and Malaya the next vulnerable. If the Japanese entered Siam it was proposed to avoid the country altogether by flying from Rangoon to Mergui, an island off the west coast of Lower Burma, then to Penang in Malaya and on to Singapore. If the situation worsened, the coast of Lower Burma could be avoided by flying from Rangoon to Port Blair or Nancowry on the Andaman Islands in the Bay of Bengal, then via Sabang and Penang to Singapore. Should Malaya be occupied by the Japanese it was intended to divert the flying-boats from Port Blair and Sabang to Padang in Sumatra, Batavia in Java, and so on to Australia. These were the three phases of what was known as the Far East "reserve route," in the event of Japanese aggression. During the middle months of 1941 these reserve routes were quietly surveyed and the necessary equipment to operate flying-boats was installed along them.

British Overseas Airways, with its ever-growing commitments, was gravely short of air crews in October 1941, and to ease the position the Qantas crews started to fly on to Karachi, to take over the flying-boats at that point instead of Singapore: Australian crews were flying, therefore, over the whole of those parts of the route which were affected when the Japanese marched into Siam in December.

When the Japanese invasion began, Mr. W.L. Runciman and Mr. J.W.S. Brancker (then respectively Director-General and Indian Regional Director of British Overseas Airways) were very nearly trapped in Bangkok, where they had arrived only a few days previously on a tour of the routes. They intended to leave on the eastbound flying-boat on Monday, December 8th, but in the early hours of that morning the resident Airways man learned that the Japanese had landed at Singora and were expected at Bangkok within two hours; the flying-boats were diverted to the reserve route, to avoid Siam altogether. That evening about 600 Japanese troops moved into Bangkok without any disturbances – the Siamese forces had already been ordered to cease resistance – and occupied the Sports Club after polite negotiations with the committee. The three Airways officials escaped from beneath their noses by the simplest possible means.

Next morning they went to the railway station, breakfasted in the restaurant, and caught the 9.50 train to Pitsanulok, in the north of the country. There they chartered two aircraft from a Siamese air line company and flew to Meh Sord, just inside the western border of Siam; bullock carts, a primitive canoe across a river and a short walk took them thence into the then safety of Burma.

By this time the second phase of the reserve route, through the Andaman Islands, was working quite smoothly, although the Airways men were disconcerted at the speed with which the Japanese advance had forced them back on to their rear defence lines. But the military value of the merchant air service was again speedily proving itself in this new theatre of war. A load of ammunition was urgently needed at Singapore. It was placed on board the flying-boat *Cassiopeia*, Captain C.E. Madge, and flown there on December 22nd.

Seven days later *Cassiopeia* started on the return journey, carrying four passengers. The reserve route was still far from completely tested, and this was the first flying-boat to use the refuelling halt at Sabang, in the Dutch East Indies. It is thought that as she took off she struck some object submerged just below the surface of the water. Her hull cracked and she flooded. She floated for a short time, and the crew, who were on the upper flight deck, were able to scramble out. First Officer Blunt ran back along the sinking hull, forced open the rear escape hatch and dived into the flooded passenger cabin. He managed to bring one woman out before the flying-boat sank, but she could not be brought round by artificial respiration; all passengers were lost.

The following day the Director of Civil Aviation in Burma temporarily suspended all flying-boat services south of Rangoon while the third phase of the reserve route was being put into operation. This route avoided Malaya altogether, taking the flying-boats farther to the west and south, through Sumatra and Java. Singapore was being bombed with increasing regularity and weight, and although the Airways headquarters remained there, a stand-by staff had been moved to Batavia, from which airport Singapore itself was served by a shuttle.

From that time onwards the Empire flying-boats, manned by Australian crews who hitherto had been flying this vital but until then comparatively peaceful section of the Horseshoe route, found themselves travelling through some of the hottest skies which merchant airmen have faced anywhere in the world war. Their tasks were not only to keep the Horseshoe Section open as long as possible, but to fly reinforcements and supplies into the worst battle zones, and to bring out crowded cargoes of women and children to safety in Australia. In the skies the unarmed flying-boats were frequently intercepted by Japanese fighting aircraft; on the waters of their anchorages they were continually bombed and machine-gunned.

The war record of the squadrons of the Royal Australian Air Force is plain proof of the qualities of Australian serving airmen; that of their colleagues of Qantas and the other air lines bears inspection as proudly.

During their flights into Singapore and along the coasts of the Dutch East Indies in the early days of January 1942, the captains developed a technique of their own for dodging air raids. Their radio officers tuned in to the radio stations of the ports which they were approaching; when they thus received news of an alert at the port, the captains put down on lonely stretches of coastal water and waited for the all-clear before proceeding. At one place a flying-boat alighted at what appeared to be a deserted harbour, and it took two hours' shouting through a megaphone before a boat could be persuaded to put out to her; her own arrival had precipitated an alarm, and the whole town had gone to cover. At another a flying-boat could scarcely alight for the crowd of native craft putting hastily down the river after the alert had sounded.

The flights into Singapore itself grew particularly uncomfortable. Often, as the flying-boats approached, their crews could see Japanese aircraft over the port, with the burst of bombs beneath them and fires spreading. On those occasions they sought temporary refuge in a little bay along the coast which, discovered by Captain Thomas, was known endearingly as "Thomas's Funk-hole." Mr. Duff Cooper, Minister of State, was brought from Singapore in mid-January and flown to England.

Throughout that month there had been little trouble in operating the flying-boats east of Batavia – it was along the coasts of Sumatra and Malaya that the Japanese fighters and bombers were on patrol. But on January 30th Corio, Captain A.A. Koch, left Darwin at dawn with a passenger-load of men urgently needed in the war area, and five crew. She intended to return from Soerabaja with women and children.

When she was 10 minutes from Koepang in the Dutch port of Timor a radio message was sent to warn her that a heavy bombing raid had started on that port. The message came a few seconds too late. Seven Japanese Zero fighters had found her, and were attacking from above and astern. Captain Koch dived to sea level, and made for the nearest beach, about 15 miles distant. The Zeros followed, maintaining accurate fire. Most of the passengers were killed in the first few bursts and the captain was wounded in the arm and leg. He threw Corio about in an effort to dodge the machine-gun bullets with greatest coolness. After each swerve he waited until the stream of tracer was again breaking the windows of his cockpit; then he swerved violently in towards them, a manoeuvre which brought the flying-boat each time out of the line of fire. He carried out these twisting movements at a height of about one foot from the surface of the water, into which the wingtip floats dipped as Corio twisted and swerved.

Some 10 miles were made towards the beach, then Corio was done. Two of her engines were on fire and she was rapidly losing speed. Koch put her down, and her nose plunged into the water, so badly holed was her planing surface. He himself was thrown over the steering column and through an opening in the cockpit. When he came to the surface he found that his first officer, his radio officer and three of the passengers had been thrown clear and were swimming round the wreck of the flying-boat, settling down with her wings then awash. The captain and one passenger, being strong swimmers, decided to attempt the five-mile swim to the beach in an effort to bring help to the others; Koch was forced to swim with only his arms, owing to the wound in his leg. After swimming for three hours they reached the breakers, and got ashore. Shortly afterwards another passenger appeared on the beach to which he had swum with the support of a mail bag; and soon two more survivors joined them, the First Officer and a passenger who had made the shore in spite of two broken ribs.

Two of the party started out for help; they returned on the evening of the next day with some food and water from a native village, which they had reached by swimming a river 400 yards wide and full of crocodiles. Afterwards one obtained a native guide and walked to Koepang, where he got into touch with the Dutch authorities and arranged for a flying-boat to pick up the rest of the party. Ten other passengers and three members of the crew had lost their lives.

The loss of Corio meant that the route from Soerabaja to Darwin had to be abandoned. The flying-boats were flown from Soerabaja direct to Broome, on the west coast of Australia. Soerabaja itself was soon being too heavily raided to permit flying-boat operations, and the northern terminal of the route had to be shifted to Tjilatjap, with another reduction of payload.

CHAPTER 12

The Break in the Horseshoe

AS THE AIRMEN were forced farther from the routes, the shuttle linking Singapore with Batavia grew less feasible. On January 30th as many British forces as could be extricated were withdrawn from the mainland on to Singapore island and the Johore causeway was blown and barricaded. Japanese air raids came more frequently, more heavily. The office of British Overseas Airways was crowded throughout the days with people seeking air passage out. In the first days of February the Japanese artillery had been moved up to the Johore shore, and shells were falling into the city; the oil installations were ablaze day and night, and oil smuts settled continuously through the noisy air.

Airways had taken the precaution of moving nearly all their equipment to Batavia while it was still possible to do so, and the Horseshoe Section was already being run from Java. Ground staff remained until the last moment before the city fell. The only considerable piece of equipment left was the Airways launch, which had to be hidden in a remote part of the harbour, since several attempts were made to steal it.

Captain W.H. Crowther brought the last flying-boat into Singapore on the evening of February 3rd. Early next morning he took off from the Inner Roads, in bright moonlight but without flares, with a load of 40 passengers. On February 6th there were definite orders that the Singapore-Batavia shuttle was to stop.

Three days later the first Japanese troops landed on the island. From that moment the unhappy story of Singapore moved rapidly; the island was surrendered on February 15th. Two days before that the Airways men plied back and forth in their remaining launch, ferrying evacuees out to some small steamers in the roads. Only one other launch was operating, or even afloat, in the whole of the Inner Roads by then, and that was sunk by shellfire.

Next day, February 14th, there were no more prospects of any flying-boats, nothing more that the ground staff could do. At noon they embarked on the Airways launch, taking in all 11 civilians and two Army officers under orders to leave, and set course down the coast. As they looked back on Singapore, they saw the whole island covered in a pall of oil smoke, except at the eastern end. Blazing buildings were dotted about the skyline.

The smoke completely obliterated the sun. Japanese bombers were still diving on to the stricken city.

Being of shallow draught, the Airways launch successfully crossed the minefields of the Straits to an island off the coast of Sumatra. As they proceeded, its crew learned to their dismay that the Japanese had landed on Sumatra itself, and captured Palembang. The east coast of Sumatra was therefore out of the question. They found a Chinese river boat to tow them some 80 miles inland, up the Indragiri river. There they handed the launch over to the Royal Navy and proceeded in an army lorry to Padang, on the west coast, whence they caught a steamer to Java and headed for Batavia, the substitute Airways headquarters, only to learn that the last flying-boat for Australia had left, and the service had stopped.

They completed the journey to Australia by ship. For while this launch was engaged in its small odyssey the Empire route to Australia had at last been cut. Once the Japanese had captured Palembang, in Sumatra, even the last phase of the reserve route became impossible. To the west, the Horseshoe Section from Durban flew as far as Calcutta, then turned back again to Durban.

To the east there was still a hard task for the merchant airmen on what remained of the route, from the Dutch East Indies to Australia. Six Empire flying-boats were east of the break. They flew more frequently and more dangerously than ever, taking war supplies and reinforcements from Australia to the battle-grounds of the Dutch East Indies, and evacuating refugees, mostly women and children, on the return journeys. In this task, of course, they co-operated with other Australian and Dutch aircraft and with the transport squadrons of the Royal Australian Air Force.

Arduous as this period was to be, it was not to be lengthy. The first operation was to fly a shuttle service from Tjilatjap in Java to Broome in Western Australia, an ocean crossing of 1,000 miles over which the first flight was made by Captain O.F.Y. Thomas. War supplies were taken north, women, children and wounded men brought south. One flying-boat flew right over a Japanese aircraft without being noticed. Others were able to rescue airmen and seamen stranded on these sunlit beaches across which war was raging. Captain O. Denny found the American crew of a missing D.C.3 on one island beach, and alighted alongside the surf to pick up and carry them to Australia. Captain E.C. Sims, in Camilla, rescued crew and passengers from a cargo ship which they had abandoned after an air attack.

There was little less danger at the southern than at the northern end of the route, for the Japanese bombers were ranging over the ports of north-west Australia with a ferocity which seemed to presage, at that time, an intended assault on the mainland itself. On February 19th a daylight raid in successive waves struck at Darwin, where Camilla lay at her moorings among the shipping in the harbour.

After the bombing two of the captains hurried to the quay, to find Camilla still afloat, but a burning ammunition ship moored so close to her that the smoke almost hid her from view of the shore. They hurried down the ramp past wounded men who were being disembarked from the Airways launch that had rescued them, and got aboard the flying-boat. There were bomb-splinter holes in her fuselage, but the engines started, so they cast off and let her drift away from the burning ship. They thought at first of trying to hide her in the mangrove swamps, but just then they heard bombing again, fairly close. They decided the air was the safest place and took off; a few minutes afterwards the ammunition ship below them exploded with great force, severely damaging the shipping around her and the wharfside buildings. They flew Camilla to Groote Eylandt, where they kept her until the following morning, when she put back to Darwin to pick up passengers and to proceed to Sydney.

By February 28th the advance of the Japanese into Java had made it impossible to continue the Tjilatjap-Broome shuttle. Two flying-boats, Circe and Coriolanus, started on the last flight from Tjilatjap. They took off at dawn, Captain W.B. Purton flying Circe, and Captain S.K. Howard, Coriolanus; the former carried some 20 women and children evacuees, the latter brought wounded men. As Coriolanus became airborne, her crew could see Circe taxying from her moorings for take-off. The two flying-boats were in radio touch with each other for the first two hours of the flight. Then nothing more was heard of Circe. Japanese aircraft, based at that time on Palembang and the island of Bali, were known to be hunting our shipping along the Java coast. It was presumed that Circe was intercepted and shot down, and that she was lost with all aboard. Two Dutch aircraft were lost in this area the same day.

A few days later the harbour at Broome was full of flying-boats – there were 15 of them on the water, mostly belonging to the R.A.A.F. but including Corinna. At half-past nine on the morning of March 3rd, 25 passengers and their baggage were waiting on the quay to go aboard her when a large number of Japanese fighters dived from the sky over the harbour with their guns firing. Since there was no defence, they raked back and forth at will over the flying-boats, which caught fire one by one, blazed up, and began to sink.

Several of them had just arrived with loads of evacuees from the Dutch East Indies, and the passengers had not yet been put ashore. Many of them were killed in the machine-gun attacks. Others leaped from the burning aircraft into a harbour that is full of sharks. It was impossible to rescue many of them, for the Japanese attack sank not only all the flying-boats, but also most of the small craft plying between them.

Captain L.J. Brain, then operations manager for Qantas at Broome, found a row-boat which, with the help of another man, he dragged down the beach and into the water. They rowed towards the flying-boat anchorage. Half a mile out they found seven Dutchmen, two of whom were supporting a young Dutch woman in a state of collapse, and a third swimming on his back holding a baby with its face clear of the water. They took the woman, the baby, and three of the most exhausted men into the boat; the others clung to its side, and all came ashore safely. Airways engineers who had been on board Corinna when the attack started, had scrambled into a dinghy; then, when the fighters opened fire on them, had dived overboard to avoid the bullets. They got ashore without harm, rescuing some more people, as did the only two luggers remaining afloat in the harbour.

With the greater part of their flying-boat fleet lost to them – Corinthia crashed shortly afterwards at Darwin, two passengers being killed and the captain and one other passenger seriously injured – the airmen of Qantas might have been thought to have come to the end of their usefulness. But that was a view they refused to accept; they had a long score to settle. One great task which awaited them, for instance, was to re-knit the chain between Australia and the Empire routes which the Japanese had broken.

The manner in which they did so will be described later. Another was to help bring to Australia the air fighting-strength which was building up for her in the United States. It was Qantas crews who first ferried Catalina aircraft for the Australian Government over the 7,733 ocean miles from the Pacific coast of America to Australia. Captain Brain brought the first, with Captain P.G. Taylor as his navigator. After that, the merchant airmen took the Catalinas directly from the assembly lines of the American factories and flew them across the Pacific after only four or five hours' check-flights. One delivery flight covered the 7,733 miles from the American coast to Rose Bay, Sydney, in only four days. Another left a Pacific island at 5 o'clock one evening and was flown direct over a route of more than 3,000 miles to Sydney in 26 hours.

Their immediate task, however, after their Empire route had been smashed and many of their aircraft destroyed by the Japanese, was to fly supplies to the Australian troops in battle on the islands north of Australia.

In September they began the long task of hauling reinforcements and supplies to and bringing the wounded back from Port Moresby, using flying-boats and land-planes alike. The land-planes joined the general fleet of transport aircraft taking supplies onward to the battle area of Buna. Each trip entailed a flight, often in bad weather, over the jagged Owen Stanley mountains; some of the aircraft dropped supplies by parachute, some landed on strips hacked from the jungle and tall grass of Papua, so close to the Japanese lines that a sharp turn had to be made on take-off to avoid passing over the enemy trenches. At moments of crisis practically all the merchant aircraft of Australia were assembled to take a hand in the job. For the campaigns in Papua could not have been fought at all without the air transports; the battles raged always at the end of an air supply-line.

The flying-boats took part in the last-minute rush of supplies to establish the Allied base at Milne Bay, from which a counter-attack by the Japanese was successfully repulsed. The flying-boats were taken by night, often through weather which would have cancelled a normal flight, to the most advanced bases, taking supplies which were used in action a few hours after they had been unloaded. They plied back and forth from northern Australia to New Guinea, and then on to the front-line positions, with their loads of fighting men and fighting material. And as they flew, one eye on the weather, the other looking for Zero fighters, somebody wrote a jingle about it, summing up the whole thing:

> For twenty hours we sailed aloft and sauntered in the sky,
> And smoked each other's cigarettes and watched the clouds drift by –
> Soldier blokes and sailor blokes a-wingin' in to war –
> A bloke to write it up and tell 'em what the fightin's for!
> Some are reading, some are sleeping, some are just a blank,
> Some are adding up the cash they owe the bleeding bank,
> Some are calculating the distance to a drink,
> But what I want to know is this – what does the pilot think?
>
> What does the pilot think about, a-sailing thru' the sky?
> Is she down a bit too low, or is she up too high?
> Is she dropping down too fast?
> Hades! Will the petrol last?
> What does the pilot think about, a-sailing thru' the sky?

CHAPTER 13

Two Ways to India

THE YEAR 1942 was a period of building up supplies against enemy thrusts, of checking the Germans in the Mediterranean and the Japanese in the East. The occupation of Madagascar, in the middle of that year, was a blow aimed at both Jap and German. It was not a campaign in which air took a great part, nor one demanding a heavy flow of material. But once the island had been occupied there was need for an air service to the troops stationed there, to carry in supplies of all kinds, and particularly to take the mail.

The flying-boat Champion made a survey flight in December 1942, from Mombasa on the Kenya coast, via Lindi to Diego Suarez, at the northern tip of the island. In January a regular flying-boat service was started by diversion of Horseshoe Section aircraft each week to Pamanzi and Diego Suarez. It is not a spectacular service, and nothing very much happens on it, but it has been said that nowhere in the world is air transport more appreciated. The garrison troops in Madagascar continued to think of the flying-boat as their one regular link with the outside world, bringing mail, passengers, equipment, and, to one unit on a small island midway to the mainland, even fresh vegetables.

But (in 1942) the main demands for air transport services outside Africa were to India, in which vast country stocks were already being laid down, as fast as the demands of other theatres permitted, against the future battles with the Japanese.

The flying-boats of the Horseshoe Section already linked Africa to India, and the north-west of India at Karachi to the north-east at Calcutta, where, after the loss of the Dutch East Indies, the line ended. This trunk route, flying with the steadiness of a main-line railway service, carried to India a valuable load of war supplies, and provided a quick means of communication with Africa and Britain for the key-men needed to build up India into a war base. There was a connection on the lake at Gwalior with the capital at Delhi, whither the RAF flew a land-plane service timed to coincide with the flying-boat arrivals. There was a further connection at Calcutta with an air line which played a great part in the Far Eastern war, the China National Aviation Company.

CNAC is really outside the scope of an account of British merchant airways, for that company is composed of Chinese and American interests; in the early days most of the air crews were Americans, but an increasing number of Chinese pilots and airmen has been introduced during the course of the war. Its ground organisation at the Calcutta terminus was handled by Indian National Airways (INA), and it was officially represented in India by British Overseas Airways. The captains of this company were already veterans at air transport in wartime. They had kept the routes open from China to the outside world, flying over wide stretches of enemy territory, in those earlier years of uneasy European peace during which China was already deeply engaged in her long struggle. They had long before developed the art, common now to all transport airmen, of dodging unarmed through cloud and darkness to avoid enemy fighters, had learned long since to think of clear blue skies or brightly moonlit nights as bad weather, of storms, thick cloud and obscurity as good.

As the Japanese advanced in the early months of 1942 through Burma, the captains of CNAC switched their routes ever farther to the north, heedless of the cruel mountain ranges which are interposed. They diverted their aircraft to assist in the evacuation of civilians, mostly women and children, from the path of the Japanese. Working with them at that time were the merchant airmen of India. The service flown by Indian National Airways for the Government of India into Rangoon was forced gradually back. INA aircraft were the last merchantmen to pull out from Mingaladon airfield at Rangoon, under heavy bombardment, bringing all the evacuees they could carry. They continued to operate into Akyab, then into Magwe, where they were joined in the work of evacuation by airmen of the other big Indian air line, Tata Airlines. Forced from Magwe, they flew to Shwebo, farther north; then to Bhamo and at last to Myitkyina. They lost one of their aircraft, but no lives, to enemy action.

When the Japanese advance was stemmed on the northern borders of Burma, CNAC set itself the task of carrying into China by air as much as it could of the war supplies that formerly travelled along the Burma Road. It had been thought that practically the same volume of supplies could go by air, and this aim was eventually surpassed, though not at first, and not by civil aircraft alone.

The two Indian air lines, meanwhile, had returned to their internal routes. On a rough division, INA operated services for the Indian Government in the north of the country, radiating from Delhi to Karachi and Jiwani, to Peshawar and to Calcutta; Tata Airlines operated similar services in the south, linking Karachi down the west coast with Bombay, Bombay through Hyderabad with Madras, and Madras through Trichinopoly with Colombo.

Tata's, organised from Bombay by the commercial house of that name, undertook with an associate company the assembly of fighter aircraft for the RAF in India. INA, organised from Delhi as the instrument of the Indian Government, provided the ground services in India for British Overseas Airways, and also operated a regular supply service eastwards from Calcutta to the rear of the battlefront in Assam. Both these companies, of course, were operated by Indians in the air and on the ground, with very few British key-men as advisers.

For the supply of India from the west the Horseshoe flying-boats were insufficient. Fortunately, an alternative route for land-planes had already been surveyed, and although it is one of the most difficult routes in the world to organise on the ground, services were opened across it by British Overseas Airways in the summer of 1942; shortly afterwards their stations were being intensively used by military reinforcement and supply aircraft. A glance at the map will show that the war trunk-line from America to the Middle East, established from the eastern cape of Brazil across the South

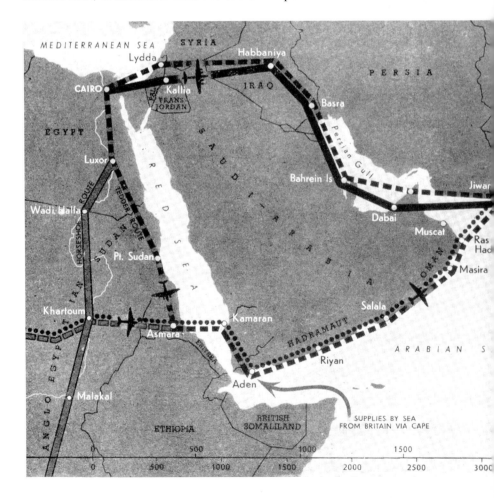

Atlantic to West Africa, and thence trans-Africa to Khartoum, if continued to India would flow naturally along the Hadhramaut coast, the southern coast of Arabia. It was precisely this Hadhramaut route which had been surveyed for the Government of India during 1941, when it was feared that the Iraq troubles might cut our Horseshoe link between Africa and India.

The surveys showed that the land-plane route could be constructed, but that the Hadhramaut coast was not suitable for flying-boats. It is desert coast fringed here and there by a few oases. In parts water is the most precious commodity. During some six months of the year the whole

Two ways to India were developed in 1942 to build up war stocks against the Japanese. The 'Horseshoe' already linked Cairo with Calcutta via Iraq. A new land-plane route was established along the Hadhramaut coast of Arabia; it was a natural extension of the America airlines coming from Brazil across Africa, and a quick transport route from the port of Aden.

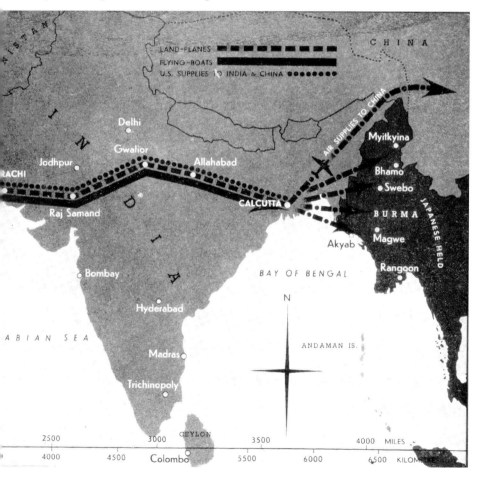

coast is unapproachable from the sea, owing to the monsoons, and long stretches of it can be reached by land only in camel trains. On some few occasions before the war, aircraft of the RAF had made flights along this coast from Aden, using small patches of hard sand as landing-grounds, but no ground organisation for a regular air service existed.

It was decided that the route should run from Aden, an old-established RAF station, eastwards through Riyan, Salalah, Masira Island, Ras el Hadd (at the eastern cape of Oman, with an emergency landing-ground at Muscat), to Jiwani on the Baluchistan coast of India, already a fully organised station of the Horseshoe Section. The RAF undertook responsibility for Aden and Riyan. The Government of India was to carry out construction of the other airfields, helped and advised by British Overseas Airways, who were to provide the ground staff and organisation. The whole cost of developing the route was borne by the British Government.

The chief tasks of British Overseas Airways were to put men, stores and equipment into Salala and Masira Island, and particularly to set up radio stations there. The job had to be done between September and May, for only at that time of the year could shipping approach the coast at all. The necessary heavy equipment was shipped to the Persian Gulf, where a tanker picked it up and carried it to Salalah. The development party, in charge of Mr. Clive Adams of British Overseas Airways, was flown at the same time to Salalah in a series of communication flights in which Tata's took a share. They arrived in October 1941 to find the tanker lying off in the roadstead, and the stores being run ashore in a dhow through heavy surf. They set up a tented camp in a coconut grove on the beach, built their bathroom and kitchen from palm-leaves, and installed the first radio station in a tent.

They were pleasantly surprised at the verdant oasis in which they had been placed. Tropical fruits grew everywhere, the water from the nearby Arab town was excellent. And their way was made much easier by the willingness with which the Sultan of Muscat, in whose domain Salalah lies, welcomed the setting up of an air route. He at once put at the disposal of the Airways men the only piece of mechanical transport in the place, his own saloon car, and shipped a three-ton lorry by dhow from Muscat to be used in building the runways. He also lent them a couple of horses. The Sultan himself was pleased to take part in one of the early experimental local flights at Salalah.

There was no disguising, however, that this was one of the truly remote places of the world. There were no postal facilities to anywhere, though messages could be sent by dhow to Muscat or Aden from September to May; during the summer monsoons the only communication with the outside world was a messenger who travelled by camel between Salalah and Muscat once a month, taking 25 days on the journey.

The only restrictions which the Sultan imposed were a few local rules which he drew up for the men at Salalah, such as: no one will leave the camp after dark except on duty; no flag of any sort will be flown; no smoking in the town or the bazaar; one of the guards will accompany any party going into the town; there is to be no music or noise for half an hour after sunset, the time of the maghrib prayer; small trees in camp garden must be duly tended.

Compared with Salalah, Masira Island was a wilderness indeed. On his first visit, Adams thought it the most desolate place he had ever seen. There was no good water on the island, nothing grew, and nothing was produced save fish; even the Arab islanders were giving the place up in despair and migrating slowly to the mainland. Nevertheless, an airfield and radio station were established on Masira. By early summer of 1942 the route was ready. It was proposed to operate an infrequent service with Lodestar aircraft from Asmara, the engineering base, to Aden, thence along the Hadhramaut coast to Jiwani and Karachi. Llandaff completed the first eastbound journey on May 11th, and for a time the British airmen flew the route once a month, a frequency that was to be increased later to once a week.

It was not only for their own use that the airmen had created this new route to India. By October the United States Air Transport Corps were pouring aircraft and supplies along it, headed for India and the Far East; for the Americans, the Hadhramaut coast route provided the necessary link in their east-about route to China. It is probably not a route which will be of first-class importance now the war is over and the European air freed from terror. But during the war it was of immense service in building up the military machine in India.

PART V

AFRICAN VICTORY

'Fortress Rock'. A BOAC Dakota silhouetted against the searchlights of Gibraltar.

CHAPTER 14

The Night Run to Malta

THE YEAR OF decisions in Africa and the Mediterranean, the year of gravest threat that was to turn to highest victory, the year 1942. The Allied and enemy armies faced each other, through spring and early summer, on a line running south through the desert from the cape of Gazala on the Cyrenaican coast. Both sides were building up supplies for another assault at the earliest moment.

The German supply lines, running from Italy and Crete across the short width of the Mediterranean, with all the railways and roads of Occupied Europe behind them, were far more easily fed than ours, which had that wide sea and air detour around and across Africa. On the other hand, the German supply lines were more vulnerable to Allied air attack than those of the Allies to the Luftwaffe. While the Allied forces were piling up strength in the desert, the RAF and Dominions Air Forces in the Middle East, together with light forces of the Royal Navy in the Mediterranean, were striking tirelessly at the enemy sea and air routes to Africa, taking a toll that was to show itself eventually in the smashing defeat of the enemy in Africa.

The chances of cutting the enemy's supply line were immeasurably enhanced by a fortress which Britain held athwart it, a fortress that had refused to capitulate to the most strenuous assault – the island of Malta. From its airfields RAF bombers could strike at enemy shipping routes far beyond the reach of aircraft based in Egypt or Libya; from its harbours light naval forces could sally in daring raids.

It was only logical that the enemy should do everything in their power to subdue that fortress. Towards the end of 1941, and throughout the first five months of the following year, the Luftwaffe flew to its assault, subjecting the town of Valletta and the half-dozen military targets on the island to the heaviest air bombardment that had then been suffered by any place in the world. There is no need to repeat here the heroic story of Malta; that is already history. But in that story the British merchant airmen wrote one chapter of their own.

It will be recalled that, in the late autumn of 1941, five flying-boats had re-formed the air link between London and Cairo by flying through the Mediterranean, directly across the enemy's battle zone. Throughout that winter these were the only civil aircraft flying to Malta, and since their primary function was to carry supplies from Britain to the Middle East, they had little accommodation for passengers or freight destined for, or leaving Malta itself. Since shipping convoys were still reaching the island, not without passing through great perils, the lack of space for Malta traffic in the flying-boats was not very important.

They used the harbour at Kalafrana, where RAF flying-boats were also stationed. It was not by any means an ideal spot, for an easterly wind brought a heavy swell into the bay. At Kalafrana were stationed the Airways ground staff of two men, a traffic officer and a ground engineer. The engineer, Mr. G.F. Soler, had worked for Imperial Airways on the island in peacetime.

When the station was closed in 1940 he preferred to stay on, being transferred to the RAF for special duties, in the execution of which, on bombarded airfields, he gained the British Empire Medal. Soler was taken back into the employ of British Overseas Airways when the flying-boat service began in 1941. The traffic officer throughout the period of the heaviest blitz on Malta was Mr. P.C. Armour, who acted as Airways station superintendent. "He has carried out his duties and rendered valuable assistance to the Royal Air Force under extremely heavy air bombardment," wrote Air Marshal (Sir) Keith Park, the A.O.C., of Mr. Armour, "in a manner which impressed members of the Service most favourably."

The flying-boats had not been visiting Malta for long before the German air bombardment started to work up to intensity; the peak was to be reached in April and May 1942. The flying-boats were so timed as to arrive at Malta after dark, to refuel and take off again before dawn. When, in full summer, the night was too short, they arrived during one night, lay hidden in a hangar all day and took off again the following night. Captain J.C. Harrington, who made many of these flights, described the approach to Malta thus: "Alighting was tricky. There was nearly always a raid on, and we were just one more in the crowd of aircraft over the island. Down at Kalafrana they put a single light out for us when they could, but usually there were too many Huns about and we had to come down in total darkness. Taking-off was just as bad. There was no waiting for the air raid to finish; you just took off when you were ready and hoped for the best."

Clare was nearly destroyed at her moorings at Kalafrana on February 3rd, 1942. A single enemy raider dived from cloud and scattered incendiaries, one of which pierced the top of Clare's hull and set fire to the chairs in her cabin. Armour quickly took a party out to her and dowsed the fire.

By early March the risks of this route, combined with the delays due to bad weather, made it uneconomical for getting supplies safely to the Middle East, and the flying-boats were therefore taken off it and sent back to the West African route. But although Malta was no longer useful as a stopping-place on the way to Cairo, the needs of the island itself could not by then be ignored. Shipping convoys bringing supplies to Malta were suffering terrible losses, and the chance that freight loaded into a ship would ever arrive was diminishing.

Yet such vital stores as cannon ammunition for the fighters and spare parts for their engines simply had to be sent to Malta by a sure route, or the island could not survive. These vital supplies reached Malta mainly by two methods, in submarines of the Royal Navy and by air transport. The latter was shared between transport aircraft of the RAF and the merchant air service. The merchantmen flew services to the island from east and from west; a night service was flown from Cairo three times a week, and another from Britain, sometimes shuttling to Gibraltar, at whatever irregular intervals could be managed.

The service from Britain was flown at first by a converted military flying-boat which had been used by British Overseas Airways on the run to West Africa. She started during March, flying from Poole to Malta (via Gibraltar) with a load of six passengers and a ton of mail and freight; the arrival of prompt air-mail at Malta during the blitz was treasured by the British troops engaged in the island's defence. Then she did one shuttle from Malta to Gibraltar and back; after that she returned to Britain. She operated in that way for several months making a turn-round at Kalafrana in a single night so long as the hours of darkness permitted, and in full summer hiding for a day at Malta between flights.

She was helped during May, when the blitz was at its strongest, by the C.W.20 land-plane Saint Louis, an aircraft which the Corporation had acquired from America, and which was then the largest twin-engine aircraft in flight; Saint Louis also made occasional flights between Gibraltar and Malta, using the airfield at Luqa. She had to be unloaded, refuelled and reloaded in a single night. These operations were always carried out during air raids, usually when Luqa airfield was itself the chief target. The only illumination was the reflection of the probing searchlights weaving among the scarlet parabolæ of Bofors shells, augmented sometimes by glare from a burning building, or the flashes of bomb explosions. The usual rule was to continue work until the searchlight cones started to move directly over the airfield, then to jump for cover as the bombs came down.

Throughout all these difficulties the air transport service was maintained with surprisingly few mishaps. Since all their arrivals and departures were made at night, the airmen were not much relieved when a reinforcement of Spitfires finally stopped the German daylight blitz on Malta after two days of fierce battle in May. That battle determined that Malta would not fall to direct assault, but left unanswered the question whether the island could be reduced by siege; all supplies were running dangerously low, every scrap of food had to be treasured, every anti-aircraft shell had to be fired on consideration. Desperate and gallant attempts by the Royal Navy to bring supply convoys into the Grand Harbour at Valletta were only partially successful. Every pound of supplies counted, and the need for air transport was more urgent than ever.

At this time British Overseas Airways opened the night route from Cairo to Luqa with Lodestar aircraft. The aircraft were flown by day to Gambut, then the main forward fighter-base of the RAF in the Western Desert; refuelling there, they set off for Malta at dusk, were unloaded and refuelled as quickly as possible, and turned straight round to fly outside the zone of worst danger before dawn.

Captain A.P.W. Cane took the first aircraft in on May 6th. He had been briefed to stand off 50 miles south of the island and wait for the all clear, should an air raid be in progress; but that was impossible, the air raid went on all night, so he came down in the middle of it. It was essential that the aircraft should be turned round within the hour if it was to be out of the danger zone by first light. Armour turned it round in 55 minutes, a time which he reduced, on later flights, to 40 minutes.

Two nights later Captain R.J.W. Barnett took the second Lodestar in. There was a heavy air raid on Luqa while it was being reloaded and although the aircraft was undamaged, the surface of the runway was littered with bomb splinters. One of these splinters punctured a tyre on take-off, the aircraft swung off the runway, the undercarriage collapsed and the machine caught fire. Passengers and crew scrambled out without injury, but the aircraft was a total loss.

This Cairo-Malta night service was maintained thrice weekly until after midsummer, flying essential aircraft spares and ammunition into the island, and ferrying out crews of transit aircraft whose machines had been destroyed or women and children from shattered Valletta. It was abandoned only when Rommel's army had pushed so far to the east across the desert that no intermediate refuelling point remained for the Lodestars; without it, they had insufficient range to reach Malta with any worth-while load.

Meanwhile every effort had been made to reinforce the services reaching Malta from the west, either from Britain or from Gibraltar. Several Whitley bombers had been seconded from the RAF to British Overseas Airways and converted into freight-carriers. It was an expedient of necessity, for the Whitleys were unsuited to the work. They had been designed to carry bombs, a load of great weight in a small compass, through the bitterly cold skies of Europe. As transports, they were expected to carry loads of much greater volume through climates that ranged from warm to tropical.

They were tried at first on the flight to West Africa, but their engines overheated so alarmingly that the experiment was discontinued. A small fleet of them was then flown from Britain to Gibraltar, to run essential freight into Malta by night. They were flown at over-load, and the captains knew that, thus laden, they could not possibly fly on one engine; engine failure meant a swift plunge into the sea, and since overheating was often suffered in the warm climate of the Mediterranean summer, an engine failure was well on the cards. With this knowledge at the back of their minds, the captains frequently set out on the seven-hour flight from Gibraltar, to arrive at Malta in the middle of heavy air bombardment.

Captain E.R. Andrews, who flew this route several times, described his first arrival thus: "It was about half-past two in the morning and black as pitch. The entire island was covered by cloud down to 800 feet, and I knew that hills reached that height on the island. We had arrived, of course, in the middle of a blitz. Searchlight beams shot up through the clouds, and I could hear the noise of the anti-aircraft guns in spite of the throb of my own engines. I flew round above cloud for two hours, waiting for instructions. I went in to land six times, and on the first five I was getting ready to touch down when I was hastily ordered up again because of obstructions on the airfield – crashed aircraft. There wasn't much pleasure in it. All the time I kept thinking that we had fighters up over the island, and that my aircraft could well be mistaken in the darkness for an enemy bomber. The worst moment came when I saw a black object dive at terrific speed just ahead of me, followed a split second later by another. I learned later that the first object was a German bomber, the second a Beaufighter which chased it right into the ground. However, we got down all right in the end.

"There was no time to turn round again that night, so we had to wait all day at Malta, a day on which the air raid warnings sounded 14 times. I got ready to take off that night, a man with a torch walking ahead of the aircraft to show me to the end of the runway. Suddenly the torch went out – another air raid. We had to scramble out of the aircraft and run for shelter in a hole in the ground, in which we huddled for 45 minutes. After that we got away."

The Whitleys were worked to capacity, as many as six of them arriving with supplies at Malta in one night. But they were not satisfactory. Apart from the risks of engine failure, each carried only one-third of the load of a Catalina and used nearly as much petrol to do so; petrol stocks on the island were falling so low that such uneconomical flying could not be continued. They were replaced in August by Hudson aircraft. By autumn the fuel position on the island was so bad that only aircraft could be employed which could fly from Gibraltar to Malta and back without refuelling. Since the British Overseas Airways fleet did not contain, at that time, sufficient aircraft of this size and range, the merchantmen had reluctantly to withdraw from the route.

In the 12 months from October 1941 to October 1942 they had carried 133,384 lb. of freight and mail, and 202 passengers into Malta; they had brought out from the island 29,422 lb. of cargo, the greater part of it mail, and 540 passengers.

CHAPTER 15

The Haul Across Africa

TO SEE THE merchant airmen's services to Malta in proper perspective it should be remembered that throughout this period their general supply tasks for the Middle East forces had also greatly increased. And these commitments had all to be met with a fleet of aircraft far too small in the first place, and, apart from the Boeings purchased from America, reinforced in an unsatisfactory manner only by a few converted military aircraft – all that Britain could provide at that critical period of the war.

The story of the air-supply routes between Britain and the Middle East throughout 1942 is one of continual struggle to carry the necessary loads in spite of a dearth of suitable aircraft. Changes were frequently made in the fleet used on the flight to West Africa, taking risks that would not be countenanced in peacetime. The three Boeing flying-boats continued to ply back and forth to Lagos as before, alternating with transatlantic flights for servicing at Baltimore. Early in the year Clare, Champion and Cathay were also placed on the West Africa route instead of the direct route over the Mediterranean. The 13 converted Whitley bombers, as has already been explained, were tried out on West Africa flights, but they could not stand the climatic conditions and had to be withdrawn.

During the summer the fleet was augmented by Golden Horn and Golden Hind. These were two Short flying-boats of the G-class, similar to the Empire flying-boats but considerably larger, which had been planned before the war for the British transatlantic service. When war broke out they had been taken over by the RAF for long-range sea reconnaissance and had served as military aircraft. By this time, however, the supply of military aircraft had improved sufficiently to allow them to be released for the work for which they had been built. They were given back to BOAC and used to reinforce the route to West Africa. So, too, were other flying-boats when the land-plane services to Malta relieved them of the necessity of Mediterranean flying.

With this fleet at work, most useful loads were being carried to West Africa; all might have been well had not disaster stepped in. On September 14th, Clare took off from Bathurst, in the Gambia, homeward-bound from Lagos. She carried a crew of six and 13 passengers, together with a heavy load of freight. Little more than an hour after she had left, she sent a radio

'First Aid'. Hoisted upon primitive scaffolding and swarming with African workmen, *Daedalus* gets rough and ready service at El Geneina during early trans-Africa days.

message to Bathurst reporting engine trouble. Twenty-five minutes later she sent an S O S, saying that fire had broken out on board. Nothing more was heard from her.

All the available aircraft in the Gambia took off to search for her, and naval motor launches set out from the coast for the spot at which she had sent her last message. They searched all next day without finding her; the following day a Catalina discovered some floating wreckage to which naval launches were guided. There were no survivors. What happened to Clare will not be known. She may have broken up on touching the water in an attempt at forced alighting, for there was a high sea running.

So ended a flying-boat which had given great service to Britain in the darkest days of the war. Her loss was as directly attributable to war causes as if she had been shot down by enemy fighters. For it was only the pressing need to carry military supplies to the Middle East which had placed her on the West Africa route. After the loss of Clare, Champion and Cathay were withdrawn from that service.

They were replaced at first by two more Catalina flying-boats from the RAF, converted military types; and later by some Liberator land-planes. By these means the volume of traffic to West Africa was maintained.

The four West African colonies had, by this time, become one of the most important air junctions of the world. They were fed from the north by the services from Britain, from the west by American transatlantic routes across which were flowing ever-increasing numbers of flying-boats, land-planes, technicians and supplies, touching down at the easternmost point of Brazil before setting out across the ocean. As well as the air-supply routes, convoys of merchant ships were putting in to the West African ports, unloading aircraft in crates and other military supplies.

From West Africa, two main routes travelled to the East: the land-plane route through Nigeria and the Sudan which was the old Imperial Airways peacetime route strengthened and developed; and the flying-boat route up the Congo and down the Nile which had been pioneered during the war by the aircraft of British Overseas Airways. Nor was West Africa the air junction for only the Middle East. Already the basic supplies for the campaigns of the Far Eastern war against the Japanese were being laid down in India, many of them passing through West Africa on the way.

To deal with all this traffic, facilities in the West African colonies had to be much developed.

At Bathurst, in the Gambia – that natural base for flying-boats, with an alighting area at the wide mouth of the Gambia river giving a three-mile run in any direction – British Overseas Airways was allotted part of the modern airport constructed for the RAF on the quay at Half Die. A few miles down the coast, at Fajara, was built a rest-house for passengers, lines of huts in a large compound across the road from the yellow beach, with a big mess-hall in the centre furnished in local red-brown mahogany. Down a little path through the bush at the back, the ground staff built a small village of wattle-huts to house the native employees and set up a farm to supply the vegetable needs of the rest-house, contriving to raise in swampland, plants which it had not been thought would grow in that climate. This settlement at Fajara was not built without difficulties; scarcely was the rest-house opened than a bomber crashed on the beach just in front of it, precipitating blazing wreckage on to the roofs of the huts, most of which were burnt to the ground, and not long afterwards another bomber crash set fire to part of the native village.

At Freetown, in Sierra Leone, a new alighting area was chosen some miles upstream in the Bunce river. Thick tropical vegetation reaches down there right to the river banks, a wall of thick greenness, in the dim recesses beneath which one can see solemn birds standing one-legged in the shallow water. All around is mangrove swamp; in the near distance towers the blueness of the mountains. At a place called Jui, on Hastings Creek which runs from the Bunce river, British Overseas Airways built their rest-house and offices.

The Gold Coast offered fewer difficulties. The airfield at Takoradi, the pre-war terminal of Imperial Airways across Africa, had been fully developed by the RAF for the assembly of reinforcement aircraft for the Middle East, while that at Accra had been likewise enlarged for the use of the Americans; the British merchant airmen used both these airfields, having merely to station a small ground staff at each.

The biggest development of all was in Nigeria. An excellent alighting area was chosen on the lagoon at Ikoyi, a suburb of Lagos, where a long jetty was run out into the water. The airfields for land-planes were lengthened and improved throughout the colony, and many smaller airfields were built, not for merchant aircraft only, but for the great stream of Allied military aircraft passing through the colony.

There has been much ill-informed talk about the airfields built in Africa to accommodate the flow of military supplies during the war. Yet the facts are quite clear. In the four British West African territories some 40 airfields, landing grounds and flying-boat stations were developed or constructed, all, in the first instance, by the RAF or by the civil Governments of those territories. In Nigeria and the Gold Coast, the two most important, the Public Works Departments (PWD) of the local Governments were employed as agents by the RAF

Those Public Works Departments deserve a tribute. That of Nigeria built 17 new, and carried out major extensions to nine existing airfields between June 1940, when France collapsed, and the end of 1943. Although the PWD was assisted in the later stages by units of the Royal Engineers, it did much of the work with most limited resources. Materials had to be carried into the hinterland, lacking any modern communications, over drying rivers. In 1942, when there was a rush to open a second land-plane route through the colony, scratch staffs were hastily collected – at one time the European staff building extensions to an airfield at Makurdi consisted of a sergeant of the Royal Engineers, a leading aircraftman of the RAF who had once worked in an architect's office, and a missionary with some knowledge of building huts. They controlled a staff of 3,000 Africans. When an extension was urgently needed to the main-line airfield at Kano, 2,000 donkeys were hired, each group of 30 donkeys being in charge of a small African boy. The panniered donkeys plied between some nearby gravel-pits and the end of the airfield, and thus the extension was laid down.

When Pan-American Airways came on to the trans-Africa route in the summer of 1941 they imported sectional buildings from the United States to build themselves an original camp, but the Nigerian Public Works Department supplied labour and materials when that camp was doubled in size the following year. This department also built the camp for the American Air Transport Command at Kano in 1942. The local Governments undertook

'Last Word'. Now the route is consolidated. Takoradi is crowded with giant aircraft. Even the petrol truck, pumping fuel into the tanks of the Ensign, is streamlined.

all the developments at the four airfields on the route mainly used by the United States Air Transport Command, at Accra, Kano, Maiduguri and Apapa, with the exception of prefabricated buildings which the Americans imported to construct their own camps, a substantial amount of electrical and radio equipment for their own use, and the hangars at Accra.

All the airfield development in West Africa for the RAF, British merchant airways or the USAAF, with the exception of portable equipment imported from the United States, was paid for either by the local Governments or by the British Government. Certain charges were made for work done for Pan-American Airways, but when that company was replaced by the American Air Transport Command, the cost of equipment which the military took over was charged to the British Government as reverse lease-lend.

It will be seen, therefore, that the development of a great air supply junction in the West African colonies, and of the air routes that led eastwards from them, was very properly undertaken, practically in its entirety, by the Governments of those colonies or by the British Government.

Those routes eastward to the Middle East war were even busier in 1942 than during the previous year. It had been hoped that Pan-American Airways, coming on to the route as far as Khartoum as agents for the United States Government in 1941, would be able to handle all the military supplies to be ferried through West Africa, so that British Overseas Airways could be withdrawn to concentrate on the section between Khartoum and Cairo. But this was not to be.

The Japanese attack on Pearl Harbour brought the United States into the war in December of that year. American forces had also to be supplied, at first in the Far East, to which one of the air transport routes lay across Africa, and later in the Middle East. With this tremendous added commitment, Pan-American Airways were unable to carry all the load; they grew naturally more and more concerned with hauling American supplies, and British aircraft had to return to the trans-Africa route to cater for British traffic. Far from being relieved of the load on this section of the Empire air supply lines, the British airmen were flying far more hours trans-Africa in 1942 than in the previous year.

There was no respite for them when the Air Transport Command of the United States Army Air Forces took over, in the August, from Pan-American Airways. For the transport aircraft of the American Air Force were similarly concerned, in the first place, with supplies for the American forces; so that although, in total, a far greater weight of material was being hauled across central Africa, our Middle East forces had still to rely largely on the British merchant airmen for their share. Towards late summer, when the task of building up for the great African campaign of the winter was at its peak, the burden on the trans-Africa route was heavy indeed.

It was somewhat relieved when, in full summer, the fleet of E-class Ensign aircraft which had been gradually flown out from Britain had been modified in order to withstand the climate, and was placed on service from Asmara via Khartoum to Lagos – Asmara was the eastern terminal because the Ensigns had their engineering base at the depot which British Overseas Airways had built there. The Ensigns, high-wing, four-engine monoplanes with a span as great as that of the Empire flying-boats, had been planned and built by Armstrong Whitworth for Imperial Airways before the war, and were intended to be the land-plane counterpart of those flying-boats for the main trunk routes. Although their standards of speed and load were pre-war, and their production has not been continued, they proved of great value as the largest transport land-plane in service.

Alongside the British and the Americans, the Belgian SABENA continued their charter land-plane services, indeed extended them to Cairo. Similarly, the flying-boats continued to ply back and forth on the water-route, the Congo and the Nile, carrying eastwards many key-men for the Middle East Forces, and returning with ferry pilots, to take over more fighters at Takoradi and to fly them across Africa to battle.

Another attempt was made to re-establish a direct Britain-Egypt service over France and the Mediterranean for the most urgent despatches,

Fajara Rest-House, Bathurst, built to meet the busy wartime traffic, is a neat compound with a big central mess-hell furnished in the local red-brown mahogany.

passengers and freight. The only aircraft then available which could make the flight without an intermediate halt were Liberator B.24 land-planes, used on the North Atlantic crossing. Two of them were detached from that service, and the first set off for Cairo direct at the end of January 1942. It reached Cairo from Hurn, in the south of England, in 11¼ hours. It made the return journey, commanded by Captain Humphrey Page, on February 15th. As it approached the shores of England the Liberator was shot down into the sea off Eddystone. Crew and passengers were all lost.

Flights were continued direct to Cairo, a few weeks later, with the other Liberator. They were maintained regularly and without mishap until the end of the year.

Among the war supplies carried between Britain and the Middle East on these various air routes was that vital commodity, troop mail. Men in the desert and their relatives at home were sometimes dissatisfied at the speed with which their letters were carried; they will accept the assurance that everything possible was done by the airmen, themselves fully aware of the importance of home letters, to carry the mail with speed on these hard-pressed services.

The volume of private mail that could be carried was gravely reduced after the Italian declaration of war, simply because the pay-load on the long hops to West Africa was comparatively small, and was urgently required for freight of high Government priority. At the same time it was fully realised how important it was for men in the Forces to be able to correspond quickly and cheaply with their families at home.

The Post Office, therefore, introduced a light-weight post card which, at a charge of 3d., was flown via West Africa to the Middle East. Not long afterwards the airgraph system was introduced, by which letters written at either end of the route on special forms were photographed on to microfilm, of such lightness and compactness that thousands of letters could be stowed away in any aircraft.

On arrival the films were enlarged and printed, and photographic copies delivered. Each letter on this service also cost only 3d., and were the films lost en route the originals were re-photographed for second despatch. The airgraphs became the staple means of communication between the men in the Forces and home. They were later supplemented by letter-cards, the postage on which was also 3d., consisting of a single sheet folded and sealed, issued to the troops on a ration basis. They were liable to travel between Britain and West Africa by sea if the military demands on the pay-load available in the air were exceptionally heavy. But every endeavour was made to send them by the all-air route, and often they proved to be the quickest means of written communication.

As more plant became available, the airgraph system was extended to the troops in India, and to most parts of Africa. Canada started an airgraph service to her troops in Britain. The airgraphs were available not only to Service men but to civilians. Later the light-weight air letter was made available, and perhaps this form of mail, created during the war for the needs of the troops, may become a staple part of post-war air-mail.

CHAPTER 16

Merchantmen at Alamein

THE GRAVEST MATTERS of 1942 were the campaigns in the Western Desert. Attacking at Gazala in May, Rommel drove the Eighth Army back from Cyrenaica, over the Egyptian wastes of the desert almost to the borders of the Delta; only on the last line of desert defence at El Alamein was he held.

It has already been shown how this enemy advance, by capturing the desert airfields at which aircraft could be refuelled, prohibited the direct air service between Britain and Egypt save to long-range Liberator aircraft, and cut the merchant route to besieged Malta; how the airmen were forced still to concentrate on the long supply detour through West Africa.

Similarly, the enemy advance threatened that network of short-haul air

The Operations Room at Almaza, the BOAC land-plane base at Cairo. The airline runs like a thread across the squared map of Africa. The white counters, marked with the names of pilots, show positions of the aircraft flying on the route.

routes which radiated from Cairo under the Tedder Plan. These services had fallen short of expectation, mainly because of engineering difficulties – a dearth of spare parts, and of personnel. The number of engineers which it was found possible to spare for Asmara was less than one-third of the number that had been envisaged; in consequence, the number of hours flown annually on these routes was something less than half that which had been proposed.

When, at midsummer, there was a suggestion that the fleet of aircraft, and the scope of the plan, should be greatly increased, it was found that Asmara would have to produce up to 1,000 aircraft engines a year, and to overhaul two airframes every three days. The men to do it simply were not available, for so many of the Corporation's technical men had been needed earlier in the war in the aircraft industry, and could not by then be released. Reluctantly, therefore, BOAC had to conclude that they could not take over the whole of the air line operations of Middle East Command, but could continue to operate only the fleet of 40 aircraft already flying on Tedder Plan routes side by side with an RAF Transport Group.

Nevertheless, on this restricted basis, the air lines were by then linking Cairo with Palestine, Iraq, Persia and Turkey to the north, with Luxor, Port Sudan, Asmara, Addis Ababa, Saudi Arabia (at Jeddah, close to Mecca), the Sudan, Uganda and Kenya to the south. The Hadhramaut route from Aden to Karachi was also part of the Tedder Plan. Most of these services were flown by L-class (Lockheed) aircraft, but another service from Cairo over the same route as the Horseshoe flying-boats followed to Karachi was maintained with Wellington bombers which were converted into transport aircraft by the Asmara engineers – not that converted bombers are ever properly suitable for air line work, but this was the best that could be managed. These services, it should be emphasised, were all flown by the merchant airmen to the requirements of the RAF; they were flown for military reasons, as part of the general war structure of the Middle East.

During the dark days of the fighting at Alamein in June and July, arrangements had to be made to continue to operate these air communications, in common with everything else, should Egypt fall to the enemy. Aircraft spares and stores were sent ahead into Palestine or into the Sudan, and all staff families were sent south. The Corporation's motor yacht, *Imperia*, was placed in position at Hurghada, just south of the Gulf of Suez, and fitted with radio gear to work the aircraft in the air. All was thus set for over-flying Cairo and, if the worst happened, for withdrawing the flying-boats from India to South Africa.

These arrangements, of course, had never to be put into practice. The British line held at Alamein. Rommel's last bid for Egypt in the first five days of September was decisively beaten. Great reinforcements of men and material were flowing into Egypt from the rear. The forces of Air Chief Marshal (later Marshal of the RAF) Tedder and General (later Field-

Marshal) Alexander were mounting for the victories of the winter.

Once again, as in the previous year, the aircraft of the Tedder Plan were marshalled to provide air transport, this time on a much bigger scale, for the Eighth Army's advance across the Western Desert. Early in November 1942 the internal African routes were largely stripped of aircraft – some were closed down altogether. Aircraft en route were recalled to Cairo by radio. The largest possible fleet, mostly of L-class and Hudson aircraft, was gathered at Almaza airfield, just outside the city, which had become the British Overseas Airways land-plane station for Cairo itself.

After the bitter struggle at Alamein the Hun had cracked, and was in full retreat across the desert. On November 10th, just after the enemy had left the place and before the minefields had been properly cleared, the first of the merchant air services to the desert, 1942 series, was operating to Mersa Matruh; shortly afterwards to Landing Ground 75 which the spearhead of the forward fighter squadrons had reached.

There were few transport tasks which the merchant airmen were not given in that great drive across the desert. As fast as the Desert Air Force surged forward, the merchant aircraft pushed forward the terminal of the com-munication flight from Cairo. The daily, and later nightly arrivals were always eagerly awaited – for they brought the mail, and the newspapers. They also brought, in large quantities, ammunition for the cannon of the fighters and dried blood for the field hospitals. At moments of urgency they brought spare tracks for disabled tanks, springs, tyres and engine spares for the M.T. trucks upon which the speed of the advance so much depended, and reinforcements of key-men. They crammed their aircraft with freight until, as one captain put it, the cabins looked more like the holds of ships; they crammed them so full that sometimes the crew could not get in through the door, and had to climb on the wings and through the windows in order to reach the cockpit.

On occasion, the unarmed aircraft operated to places far behind the enemy lines. Early in the campaign, as the Eighth Army pushed well into Libya, a detachment of Hurricane fighters was sent to a secret landing ground far south in the desert, well behind the enemy's forward positions, in order to shoot up the supply traffic hundreds of miles to the rear on the coast road between Benghazi and El Ageila. The operation lasted for only a few days, but during that time some of the supplies the fighters needed – including such oddities as a bale of camouflage netting and a despatch rider complete with his motor bicycle – were flown to them at their desert hide-out by merchant aircraft.

As the communication line was stretched by the speed of the advance the return journey from Cairo to the desert could be managed in a single day only by taking off from Almaza before dawn and alighting there after dark. Day after day, with little respite, the airmen maintained those long hours of desert flying, often through extremely bad weather, with a cheerfulness founded on the feeling that they were playing their part in the tremendous African victory. By mid-November they were flying to Gambut, that vast dusty series of fighter airfields scraped from the top of the plateau near Tobruk; a few days later they were on to Tmimi, then Martuba, on the edge of the Djebel Akdar and radiating then to Msus, far south in the desert, or El Magrun, littered with wrecks of enemy air fuel-carriers, on the coast below Benghazi.

Early in December the route ran to Benina, the big Italian airfield, shattered by incessant bombing, outside Benghazi itself. Nor was it only in the air that the merchant air service played its part in the desert campaign. Pushing forward with the advance units of the Desert Air Force went Airways engineers and traffic men, living in tents as the men of the Services lived – and as the air crews were forced to, when the route grew too long to be flown back and forth in a single day.

Still the advance went on, and still the merchant airmen clung to it. Men in the front line who received a new track for their tank, and with it a copy of the Cairo newspaper, owed both to them. The speed with which their mail came up to the desert, or returned to Cairo for onward flight to their families was due also to them. The Luftwaffe had been beaten practically out of the sky, so air transports flew through little danger of enemy air interception; but they flew through some astonishingly bad weather, and on the ground they suffered the same hazards as everybody else.

On Christmas night, camping on the edge of a minefield at the Marble Arch airfield in Tripolitania, one of the captains was wounded by a mine that exploded just outside his tent. In January the route extended to a dusty airfield near Buerat-el-Hsun, then to Darrugh, and at last, on January 23rd, only a few hours after the enemy had left, the first merchant aircraft put down with its load on Castel Benito, the airfield of Tripoli.

The Eighth Army from the east, and the First Army and the American forces from the west, were then converging towards the grim battles of Tunisia. Once the Mareth lines had been broken the air communication route was extended, first to Gabès, then to Sfax. The captains fervently hoped to run to Tunis itself, but by that time the needs of the Middle East routes had grown more pressing than those of the desert; in May they were ordered to return to those more humdrum but no less vital tasks.

During seven months on this Western Desert service the merchant aircraft had carried 7,166 passengers – mostly senior officers or reinforcements outwards, and wounded men inwards – and 640 tons of freight. Air Chief Marshal Sir Sholto Douglas wrote to the BOAC Regional Director to express "the appreciation and admiration of the Royal Air Force" for these services. "The knowledge that supplies, reinforcements, news and mail were being delivered regularly contributed in no small measure to maintaining the morale of our fighting forces at that high level which resulted in the Axis forces being flung out of Africa."

PART VI

ATLANTIC STORY

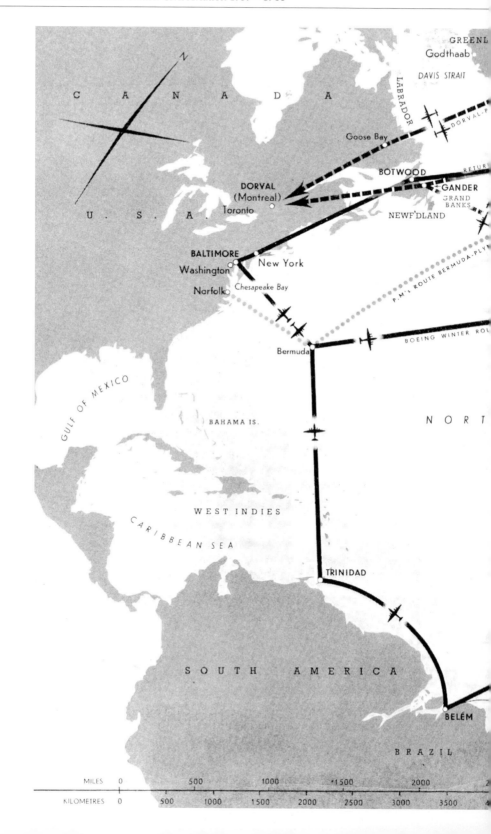

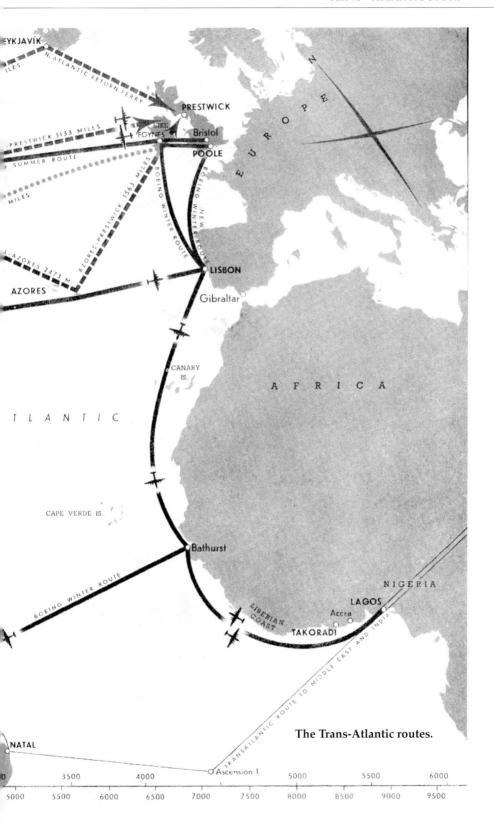

The Trans-Atlantic routes.

CHAPTER 17

High Hazard

ON JUNE 14TH, 1919, Captain John Alcock and Lieutenant A. Whitten Brown took off from St. John's, Newfoundland, in a Vickers Vimy biplane and flew 1,890 miles to Clifden, Galway, completing in 15 hours 57 minutes the first non-stop crossing of the North Atlantic Ocean in an aircraft.

During the next 15 years there were several transatlantic flights, each of which was hailed with wonder by the peoples of the world. The pilots who made those flights became international celebrities, figures of importance in the adult world, heroes to be worshipped by youth.

Ten years later some dozen captains of British Overseas Airways had flown the North Atlantic more than 50 times each, some of them climbing steadily towards the century. Those flights were made on regular merchant services, matters of routine. It is doubtful whether many people could name even two or three of those captains.

That is the measure of the conquest of the Atlantic air, that is the significance of this story.

First across. On June 14th, 1919, Captain Alcock and Lieutenant Brown flew from Newfoundland to Ireland in 16 hours. Their aircraft, the first to cross the North Atlantic non-stop, was a specially prepared Vickers Vimy bomber.

It might be thought nothing but the logical sequence of events, that once the route had been pioneered it would become commonplace as a matter of course. But to make one spectacular flight after long preparation, seizing a favourable moment of weather and without pay-load, is an achievement of one kind; to establish a regular air service over such a route is quite another, an achievement less spectacular but of vaster importance and proportions. The individual flights were daring gambles against the elements; the regular service was the conquest of them.

The story of the Atlantic conquest is something of which the British people are not yet sufficiently informed, yet it is a story of which they may feel immensely proud. The merchant captains of the British Isles, handicapped as they were in wartime, led the whole world in the Atlantic air. The establishment of regular services across that ocean was achieved by harmonious collaboration between the merchant airmen of Britain, the United States and Canada, together with the military airmen of those countries. But for the first two winters the only flag to fly on regular two-way service of the most difficult route of all, the direct North Atlantic route, was the civil air ensign of Britain; in the third winter it was joined, on regular service, only by that of Canada.

The transatlantic air route holds the same appeal to the imagination as did the shipping routes upon the surface of that ocean. Across its grey expanse, at once the barrier and the link between the Old World and the New, plied the biggest, the most spectacular ocean passenger-ships. Its waters touch on either side the greatest centres of commerce of the world, the deepest reservoirs of power, of intellect – Europe and America. For the aircraft, its skies hold some of the greatest hazards.

There are three possible air routes through those skies. The northern route stretches between Labrador and the north-eastern capes of Canada, over Greenland and Iceland to Britain. The direct route follows, very roughly, the 50th parallel of latitude between Britain and Newfoundland. The southern route reaches from New York, through the islands of Bermuda and the Azores to the west coast of Europe.

The advantage of the northern route is that it largely avoids adverse headwinds, since it circumnavigates the main depression tracks of the Atlantic. But although the winter skies over the ice-cap of Greenland itself are reasonably clear of cloud-masses laden with ice, the coasts of that desolate country, and the approaches to it, are cumbered by fog, thick cloud, and strong katabatic winds blowing down from the ice-cap, laden with heavy drift-snow and reducing visibility to a few yards. On the surface, the ice-pack of East Greenland creeps round Cape Farewell in January, advancing up the west coast and usually gripping it until late summer, though north of Goethaab the bays and inlets show streaks of clear water as early as May. The ice-pack of the Davis Strait flows down to the coast of Labrador by November, and those harbours are not navigable again until July.

The direct route from Britain to Newfoundland lies wholly within that region of the Atlantic where blow the vigorous cyclonic storms of temperate latitudes. Aircraft crossing from east to west must nearly always encounter headwinds, sometimes reaching a strength of up to 100 miles an hour. They must also encounter at all times of the year vast masses of cloud piled like the peaks of a mountain range along the whole route, cloud which tends to increase the farther the aircraft proceed to the west, and in which lurks the peril of ice to form on the wings and hull. Over the Grand Banks and the coasts of Newfoundland itself, they must contend with one of the foggiest areas of the world, though the interior of the island is relatively free. During the winter months, they must expect to find their Newfoundland stations covered in snow, with the probability of thick snowstorms whirling through the sky; the waters upon which flying-boats descend start to freeze in November, and they will not be clear of ice until May.

The southern route, though it is the longest, has happier climates. Fog is rare, the clouds stay high over the intermediate islands, though between New York and Bermuda there are likely to be three or four tropical cyclones each year, moving north-west from the Caribbean Sea, curving over the Gulf of Mexico or the West Indies, and heading to the north-east across the Atlantic.

The weather conditions of the Atlantic routes have been thus described in some fullness because the conquest of the North Atlantic air was based firmly upon meteorology. Without years of patient study by the weather men, the Atlantic could not have been conquered at all, or only at a far higher cost in men and aircraft than was actually the case.

When, at a conference in Ottawa in 1935, it was decided to project a transatlantic air service, the first step taken was to set up a meteorological organisation to probe the way. The British Air Ministry provided the staff in Eire – Foynes, on the River Shannon, was chosen as the eastern station – and at Botwood in Newfoundland, under the auspices of the Government of that country. The meteorological division of the Canadian Department of Transport saw to the western end, placing a staff on St. Hubert airfield at Montreal. Radio staffs and equipment were installed at Foynes, Botwood and Montreal, and a whole winter was spent in the laborious calibration of the direction-finding apparatus.

There were not many of these weather men, nor had they much public money to spend. Aided by frequent weather reports from shipping on the Atlantic, for the pre-war system of meteorological information was one of the finest examples there have been of selfless internationalism, these few specialists attempted by their own researches to learn something about

Alcock and Brown taking off in their Vimy from Newfoundland, June 14th, 1919.

Atlantic weather, not on the surface of the ocean, but thousands of feet up into its skies. It was a subject on which little was known.

Some of the weather men went to live at out-stations in Newfoundland. One of the British staff spent a year in northern waters aboard the S.S. *Manchester Port*, measuring the upper winds over the Atlantic and gathering data on cloud heights and types, and such matters. The information that was obtained was collated and studied on both sides of the Atlantic, until the weather men thought they could depict on paper, with fair certainty, the weather conditions that an aircraft would find over the whole route between Britain and Newfoundland. This could be done, of course, only by frequent and immediate exchanges of information between both ends of the route, and the radio service devoted to Atlantic meteorology found itself dealing daily with between 10,000 and 12,000 words of code messages.

By June 1937 everything was ready for putting theory to the test of flight. The Pan-American Airways flying-boat *Clipper III* from the west, and Imperial Airways flying-boat *Caledonia* from the east were to attempt simultaneous crossings. On July 4th the meteorologists at St. Hubert, Botwood and Foynes all began to prepare meteorological flight schedules – final statements in words, statistics and diagrams, which are handed to the captain just before he takes off and purport to show him in detail the weather he will meet at every stage of his flight.

The Atlantic had been divided into two zones, the westerly being allotted to the meteorologists of Newfoundland and Canada, the easterly to those at Foynes. In the west the weather seemed favourable, and moderate west winds were forecast at a height of 10,000 feet. The information at Foynes was not so encouraging, the meteorologists foreseeing much low cloud, rain and quite strong headwinds.

Clipper III was given a take-off time of 21.00 hours G.M.T., and *Caledonia* of 18.00 hours G.M.T. on July 5th: both flying-boats took off on time. *Clipper III* set course on the Great Circle route at 10,000 feet, Caledonia on a rhumb line at between 10,000 and 12,000 feet. (A Great Circle course is the shortest distance between two points on the earth's surface; it may be obtained by stretching a string between the two points on a globe, but not, of course, by stretching a line between them on a flat map of Mercator's projection. A rhumb line course is that between two points which cuts all the parallels of longitude at the same angle.)

At 12.00 hours G.M.T. on July 6th *Clipper III* came into the eastern, and Caledonia into the western zone. Caledonia alighted at Botwood at 10.00 hours G.M.T., by which time *Clipper III*, having had the advantage of the prevailing wind, was already water-borne at Foynes.

The first test of the weather theory which had been studied so laboriously was reasonably successful. In most particulars, the forecasts had been accurate, particularly in the force and direction of the winds. The amount of cloud had been much under-estimated.

Imperial Airways made another survey flight across the Atlantic that year with *Cambria*; on the return journey, she put up the then record time of 10 hours 33 minutes from Botwood to Foynes. A regular service had also been started between Bermuda and New York, a service interrupted by the loss at sea of the flying-boat *Cavalier*, which could not be replaced. In the following year experiments were made with the Short-Mayo composite aircraft, in which the lower component, *Maia*, took off with the upper, *Mercury*, on her back, launching her with a full load of petrol in mid-air. In this manner, on July 20th-21st Mercury reached Montreal, after a non-stop flight from Foynes, in 20 hours 20 minutes, with a pay-load of 1,000 lb.

On August 5th, 1939, Imperial Airways started the first British North Atlantic air-mail service to Canada and the United States. The two

Pick-a-back experiment. The Short-Mayo composite aircraft, in which *Maia* launched *Mercury*, non-stop to Montreal, with a full load of petrol in mid-air. *Maia* was later destroyed in an air raid: *Mercury* joined the R.A.F.

flying-boats *Cabot* and *Caribou*, later to be destroyed by enemy action off Norway, were used for the 1939 flights. They carried no passengers, and in order to get off the water with their load of mail they practised "flight refuelling" – that is, they took on board the extra amount of petrol they needed from a tanker aircraft in flight beside them. Harrow aircraft were used as tankers at Foynes and Botwood. Flight refuelling was carried out in this manner:

The First Officer and Radio Officer wound out a grapnel on a long cable from the flying-boat's tail. The *Harrow* formated to starboard and fired another cable by rocket, to catch on the grapnel of the first. A hosepipe was then wound out on the cables from the *Harrow* to the flying-boat and drawn tight into an airproof fitting. The *Harrow* climbed above the flying-boat and released 800 gallons of petrol through the hose, through which nitrogen has previously been forced to prevent electric discharge, the officers in the flying-boat controlling the operation by flag signals at the window. The contact point was then flooded with anti-fire substance and contact broken, the *Harrow* reeling in the hose and returning to base. The whole operation took up to 20 minutes, during which time the flying-boat was already proceeding on her course.

During the year, *Cabot* and *Caribou* made eight round trips across the Atlantic, flying a distance of some 50,000 miles without mishap. Pan-American Airways, from their side, had already begun a weekly trans-atlantic service during the summer months. The British services were still in progress when war broke out, and were completed to schedule. Once war started, and the American Neutrality Act was passed, the American Clippers could fly only to Eire, not to Southampton, and we had to run shuttle services to pick up at Foynes the passengers whom the Americans carried.

CHAPTER 18

The Twenty-Nine-Hour Day

ON APRIL 24TH, 1940, the Air Minister was compelled to announce in the House of Commons that the British could not expect to operate a trans-atlantic air service that year, as the aircraft had been diverted to defence purposes. *Cabot* and *Caribou*, indeed, together with the G-class flying-boats which had been built to augment them, had been handed over to Coastal Command of the RAF.

This was a bitter disappointment to the merchant air service; they had hoped to establish, in wartime, a chain of British routes from New York to Auckland, the longest in the world. Soon afterwards it was determined to try the Atlantic route with aircraft not specially adapted for it, giving them extra tank-space so that they might make the journey without flight refuelling. The aircraft chosen and prepared were the flying-boats *Clare* and *Clyde*. The boldness of this decision is emphasised by the fact that it was made on the day before the final capitulation of France. The decision was influenced by the particular need of the service for the Ministry of Aircraft Production.

On August 3rd, *Clare* took off from Poole, touched down to refuel at Foynes, and set course to the west that night on the first of the 1940 flights. Her pilot was Captain J.C. Kelly Rogers, and his crew were Captains E.R.B. White and E. Rotherham, Radio Officers J.L. Burgess and C.E. Wilcockson. She left in complete secrecy. Nothing was said to the world until, after an uneventful flight of 15 hours 32 minutes, she alighted at Botwood the following morning. Then indeed there was a story to tell. At a crisis in the war, when France had fallen, Italy had struck, and all Europe lay under the domination of the enemy, Britain had not only found aircraft capable of flying the North Atlantic, but in doing so had started the first British North Atlantic passenger service. For in addition to mail and Government freight, *Clare* carried three passengers, two Government officials and a representative of the Secretary of the United States Navy.

Clare proceeded to Montreal and New York, arriving there at dusk the same day, August 4th. Her arrival created much excitement in the newspapers of America and Britain, and New Yorkers went down to see her, lying calmly at her moorings, the camouflage on her wings and hull the only evidence of war. Two days later her sister ship, *Clyde*, was to take off on that long flight to the West Coast of Africa which would link

Britain once again with her overseas air routes to the south and the east.

Clare left New York, homeward bound, on August 8th, bringing with her a Treasury official and the first party of American pilots who had been engaged by the Ministry of Aircraft Production to join Air Transport Auxiliary and ferry military aircraft from factory to squadron in this country. She crossed the Atlantic, with favourable winds, in 12 hours 59 minutes, and arrived at Poole on August 10th.

Four days later, under the command of Captain J.T. Kirton, with Captain J.S. Shakespeare as co-pilot and Captain T.H. Farnsworth navigator, this last being the only one who had made the Atlantic crossing before, *Clare* began her second outward journey. One of her four passengers was Captain Harold Balfour, Under-Secretary of State for Air.

It was a rough crossing. For eight hours after leaving Foynes she flew through rain and low cloud, into the teeth of such a strong headwind that for a time the captain thought he would have to put back. She flew low to avoid the wind as much as possible. Some of the time she was only 450 feet above the surface of an ocean so lashed by wind that whitecaps were visible even through the rain. At about 9 o'clock next morning the luck changed. *Clare* flew through a weather front, catching all the bumps, but found behind it an east wind which blew for three hours, increased her ground-speed from 89 to 150 knots, and knocked an hour and a half off the total flying-time for the journey. She took 16 hours 44 minutes to reach Botwood from Foynes, and then proceeded to Montreal and New York, alighting at La Guardia airport just as dusk fell on August 15th.

She brought the mail and six passengers back from New York on August 18th. While she was in flight, her sister ship, *Clyde*, dropped down on to the Congo river at Leopoldville, and set ashore the French general who was to swing Central Africa to the Allied side.

She made the third crossing at the end of August, arriving home again on the day before the Luftwaffe's attack on the Surrey docks heralded the all-out onslaught on London. Her fourth crossing, that which was described in the opening chapter of this account, carried to America at the peak of the Battle of Britain a message of reassurance from these islands. *Clare* was then switched to the new route to West Africa, and *Clyde* took her place on the Atlantic for the fifth and last Atlantic service of 1940.

When she had moored up in Poole harbour on October 11th, the British airmen contemplated her with satisfaction at the achievement. There had been, it is true, only five return flights. But the British passenger service had been flung across the North Atlantic skies during the worst year of Britain's war, and in spite of the fact that the flying-boats specially adapted for the task had been lost on active service. Moreover, the two Atlantic flying-boats *Clare* and *Clyde* had also, in those desperate days, re-knit the link to West

Close-up of a giant. In 1941, three Boeing 314A flying-boats were bought from the United States to strengthen the Atlantic routes. Here we can see the massive tail-plane and fuselage of one of them, showing the stepped windows of the cabins.

Africa between Britain and the Empire routes; the British service had, after all, created the longest chain of passenger-carrying air routes in the world, from New York to Auckland.

Next year there was considerable change in our North Atlantic services. In addition to a ferry service with land-planes which is shortly to be described, three new flying-boats came into the picture. When the Under-Secretary of State for Air crossed to America in *Clare*, he took the opportunity to purchase reinforcements for the British merchant air fleet, since it was then out of the question for our own aircraft factories to be diverted to such construction. He bought three large Boeing 314A flying-boats to be delivered early in 1941.

These flying-boats were bought by the British Government for cash, and were not supplied under the lease-lend arrangement. The British held permits from the United States Civil Aeronautics Board to fly a commercial air service transatlantic to New York, but British Overseas Airways told the Civil Aeronautics Authority that these three Boeing flying-boats would not be used on any commercial transatlantic service, but for purely official purposes.

They were bought primarily in order to strengthen the route between Britain and West Africa. It was to be found, however, that they needed

The BOAC's Boeing Model 314A Clipper G-AGCA, *Berwick*, pictured landing on Lagos Lagoon, Nigeria, for moorings at the West African flying boat terminal at Iquoi during the Second World War.

certain engineering overhauls after every 120 hours' flying. Since servicing of the Boeings is highly specialised, and draws on some 14,000 different spare parts which must be bought from a number of different firms in America – and since no facilities existed in wartime Britain for such intricate work – the aircraft were flown back to the United States for overhaul after each shuttle between Britain and West Africa.

In this way grew up an intermittent transatlantic service, the only one Britain flew in 1941 with flying-boats. Obviously the aircraft did not make the journeys empty. They carried to full capacity Government freight, mail and passengers, but those who travelled in the Boeings were only those whom the Government wished to travel to help the war effort, and they travelled free.

Captain Kelly Rogers was placed in command of the Boeing Flight, and in January 1941 he left for America with four other captains and their crews, to take over the new flying-boats and receive instruction on them. Pan-American Airways, from whom they had been bought, were extremely helpful, and their airmen gave ours the necessary training. The three Boeings were named Bristol, Berwick and Bangor. The first of them, Bristol, was handed over to the British airmen in April 1941. They flew her out from New York on May 22nd, travelling via Bermuda and Lisbon to Foynes. Four days later she took off on her first flight to West Africa, returning to Foynes in July with 44 passengers in addition to her crew, and 800 kilos of mail. Those figures give an idea of the size and capacity of the Boeings.

By full summer all three Boeings had been delivered, and were on service. The Flight was based at Baltimore, Maryland, whither an Airways staff was sent to man an airport at the top of Chesapeake Bay. This airport, a compact set of buildings and hangars against the dockside skyline of a great port, with a long jetty directly alongside which the flying-boats could moor, was hired from Pan-American Airways; in this respect as in all others, this company made every effort to help British Overseas Airways with the operation of the Boeings.

Until October Bristol, Berwick and Bangor flew from Britain to West Africa on the route Foynes, Lisbon, Bathurst and Lagos. After each homeward journey to Britain, they made return flights from Foynes to Baltimore via Newfoundland. Thus, they alternated a return trip to West Africa with a two-way crossing of the Atlantic.

But in winter the direct route over the Atlantic was no longer feasible for flying-boats. Even discounting the force of winter gales from the west, the waters at Botwood froze over. Captain Rogers therefore took one of the Boeings across the South Atlantic, and surveyed the winter route which they all followed until Botwood was clear of ice the following summer. These routes formed a kind of round tour in a series of loops. After engineering overhaul at Baltimore, the Boeings flew through Bermuda and Lisbon to Foynes; then south, via Lisbon and Bathurst to Lagos; then north to Bathurst; then they struck out westwards across the South Atlantic, via Belem in Brazil, and through Trinidad and Bermuda to fetch up once more at Baltimore.

Although hundreds of people have already made these transatlantic flights as passengers, and the routes are as safe and sure as any in the world, a description, written in 1944, of a typical flight might be of interest, before such things become, in post-war years, a commonplace:

> The wartime passengers gather at Airways House, by Victoria Station in London, where a Pullman train waits to take them non-stop to Poole, Dorset. There they are shepherded into a restaurant in what was once a pottery factory, close by the quay, and is now the terminal building for the flying-boat services out of Britain. At intervals, they are called out individually, to pass through the censorship and security investigations of wartime, and when all are through they embark in a fast launch, manned by young women in blue trousers and sea-jerseys who make this their wartime work, to drive swiftly past a little jetty on to the waters of the open harbour, where the flying-boat *Golden Hind* (this flying-boat was later transferred to Durban for services to Madagascar, Seychelles, and over the Indian Ocean, and the Boeings flew to Poole) rides at her moorings in a stiff breeze. It is her function to ferry the load across to Foynes.
>
> This preliminary flight is not very interesting, for by wartime regulation all the windows are covered with fixed white curtains,

through which the reflected light from the water shimmers on the cabin roof, as the flying-boat casts loose and taxies for take-off. *Golden Hind*, stripped of all her luxury fittings, contains nothing but banks of seats ranged upwards into the tail, something in the manner of a sharply pitched theatre gallery.

The passengers – some Government officials, a few scientists perhaps, a diplomat or two, some serving officers in civilian clothes, possibly a few women – begin cautiously to make each other's acquaintance. Soon the flying-boat is passing at a low height over the green and yellow of the Eireann fields, white cottages and farmhouses tucked into their corners; Tipperary goes by, Limerick comes into the captain's view, with the curves of the Shannon. She puts down on Shannon water by the small stone quay at Foynes, with the green hills rising behind, a stack of cut timber near the customs and immigration sheds, a few Eireann army officers in their green-khaki uniforms. The great bulk of Berwick rides at her moorings in the river, together with a couple of American flying-boats.

After dinner in the whitewashed, thatched village of Adare, the passengers drive down again to the river quay, noting each break in the clouds to the west, and embark in the launch for Berwick. It is the first time most of them have seen a Boeing. Technically, she is a high wing, four-engine monoplane flying-boat of 40 tons; a better idea of her size is to say that four large launches can come alongside her simultaneously, that she has a wing-spread of 153 feet, and that on shorter flights she can carry up to 60 passengers, although transatlantic she takes about 25. She carries a crew of 11.

She has no wing-tip floats, but is stabilised on the water by a sponson protruding from her hull at either side at water-level. These sponsons, resembling a pair of short, thick wings, serve also the purposes of carrying fuel and acting as embarking platforms for the passengers, who walk from the launch across them to enter the wide door in the flying-boat's side. This leads straight into the midships cabin, in peacetime the saloon where drinks are served from a bar, but now a dining and smoking-room, with seats ranged around four tables.

Forward is the purser's office, and a couple of cabins reserved for those of the crew off watch, with a small pantry for the steward to port, and a well-equipped washroom to starboard, with running hot and cold water. Aft there are three more cabins, open to a central corridor, each holding eight passengers; the corridor leads to an enclosed cabin in the tail which, in peacetime, was the 'honeymoon suite.'

All this is on the lower deck. The aircraft is worked from the upper, the flight deck, where the crew are already settling down in this spacious compartment to arrange maps on chart tables, set out the instruments of navigation, open up contact on the radio equipment; the captain and his first officer have probably taken their seats in the cockpit forward; the engines are started, and one radio officer, earphones on his head, stands in an open hatchway in the nose, ready to cast off.

She lifts easily from the water. Soon it grows dark and there is nothing to be seen through the windows. Curtains are drawn, lights lit. Passengers gather in the midships cabin to smoke, talk, or read one of a bundle of magazines. One of the stewards busies himself turning the seats into bunks, drawing curtains before each in the manner of a railway sleeping-car; one by one the passengers go to bed.

But there is no sleep for the captain or his first officer, though the others of the crew have short watches below. They have set course on the Great Circle from Foynes to Botwood, flying into a headwind of 30 knots, rather more than they had anticipated. Berwick is flying steadily at 2,000 feet – what motion there is resembles that of a motor coach on a smooth road more than any other sort of transport. She alters course only slightly now and then, to avoid cloud masses in which there may be ice.

For a time the navigator has sight of the stars overhead, and sometimes of the sea beneath him if he wishes to drop a flare to calculate his drift. But half-way through the night the weather closes right in, no sight of sea or sky, nothing but blackness. Through his radio officers the captain is in touch, if he wishes, with friends on the ground at either end of his route, friends whose delicate radio detection-apparatus plots his position every mile of the way; but sometimes he has no need of them, navigating by dead reckoning. Neither he nor the first officer sleeps. Shortly they will approach 'the point of no return', after which there will be insufficient petrol in the tanks to turn back to Britain and there will be no alternative but to proceed.

As this point nears, they consider intently the position they have reached, the strength of the headwind, the weather forecast ahead of them; they decide to continue.

Although, if they have not altered their watches, it is quite late when the passengers awake, there is still darkness beyond the windows. The sun is racing behind Berwick, overtaking her slowly, but she is giving him a good run for it. Even when dawn comes, it comes almost imperceptibly, and for a while a violet half-light hangs outside the aircraft.

A passenger seated at the midships window sees above him the stretched spread of the port wing, its propellers tracing two almost invisible circles ahead of the nacelles, and below the stubbier expanse of the sponson, looking hard and solid, yet of a peculiar greyness in the half-light. Beads of rain slide horizontally across the window, the only indication of speed, for beyond the wing-tips wreathe only shapeless, inconsequential outlines of cloud and mist, attempting sometimes to develop some more definite form, but abandoning the attempt when it is but a quarter made and rolling off again into shapelessness.

As the light clears, the nearest approach to the definite in this aimless world is a white line of fog, lying far off to port over a hidden sea. The passenger turns from the window to the microcosm of the warm, lit cabins, to the business of toilet, of the first cigarette, of the steward bustling in with a large pot of tea, produced seemingly from heat self-generated in this small, cribbed world travelling through indeterminate and foggy space. The steward, obviously by nature a conjurer, produces from his tiny galley scrambled eggs, hot coffee, toast and marmalade, served on light-weight, plastic dishes, eaten with feather-weight cutlery. The morning drags on into more desultory reading and conversation, a game of cards perhaps, a chess match.

From the flight deck the captain, sleepless of eye, sees the first thin coastline of Newfoundland, and comments approvingly to the navigator. The radio officers make contact with the ground. The steward draws down all window blinds, by that same wartime regulation. Seats are taken, safety-belts fastened, cigarettes stubbed out. There is the feel of Berwick being eased down, a bump or two, the incredibly slight swish as her hull touches water, a small shudder, a noise as of something ripping; then she is taxying swiftly over the waters of the Bay of Exploits, anything between 15 and 17 hours after taking-off from Foynes.

A launch carries the passengers to the low shore of the bay, studded with the dark green of conifers, with wooden buildings and huts, with hangars and the litter of aircraft, with small wooden jetties. They arrive at a camp built of army huts, the ground before them neatly marked out with whitewashed stones, and even some attempt in this hostile climate at gardening – a few small Christmas trees, an optimistic row of sweet peas, and brightly coloured flowers in the window-boxes. There is the Caribou Club, stove burning, radio playing, in which to take a drink; a large wooden restaurant in which to eat lunch.

Then out to the flying-boat again, a pause of only an hour in all, to take off for the mainland of America. It does not do to pause for longer, for rain is blowing up and the clouds shutting down on the hills beyond the bay. There is nine hours more of flying to do, flying through ever-brightening weather, with glimpses here and there of a coastline away to starboard. Meals appear and disappear – there seems an extraordinary number of meals in this 29-hour day.

Towards the end, as dusk falls, it grows appreciably warmer (were this winter, it would grow infernally colder). Once more she eases down from the sky; there is a glimpse of brightly lit streets below, of a skyline of wharves, ships and cranes, and she is riding easily on the thick, slightly swelling, somewhat oily waters of Chesapeake Bay, being towed slowly backwards till she lies alongside the jetty. The passengers step ashore into America through a long, wire-netted corridor patrolled by United States police officers in shirt-sleeves, truncheons swinging; into a succession of small, brightly lit rooms to satisfy the various wartime formalities of entrance, to sip iced drinks offered by uniformed girls, each man to light his last, treasured cigarette. Once more the Atlantic has been flown. And there seems something particularly appropriate in this wartime arrival at Baltimore – an arrival, not at any glittering metropolis, but at a busy, workaday port, a place of ships, wharves, factories, night shifts, production, and the strong smells of industrial process."

The three Boeings flew journeys of this sort with excellent regularity and lack of incident. They reduced the high adventure of an Atlantic flight to the level and safety of a railway journey. There were delays now and then when weather forbade take-off, but they were neither frequent nor lengthy. Alternating with the Atlantic crossings they flew to West Africa, and it was on one of these flights that occurred the only incident sufficiently out of the usual to make a story. Flying Berwick off the Liberian coast in West Africa Captain Gordon Store sighted a small craft, evidently a ship's boat, full of the survivors from some U-boat attack. As he circled and came low over the boat its occupants, some of them women, held up a board on which they had chalked, "S O S ... Water."

There was no container aboard Berwick which could be used for dropping water, so the crew filled a double pillowslip with fresh fruit and a can of orange juice, adding a waterproof bag containing cigarettes, matches and a note of encouragement, tied the whole thing to a lifejacket and dropped it close to the boat; a man was seen to jump over and bring it safely into her. Then a radio message was sent to shore, and ships came out to rescue the survivors.

There were few such incidents to ruffle the monotony of these Atlantic and West African flights. The Boeings flew – as they still fly – stolidly over the course, returning each time for servicing in the big hangar and on the slipway at Baltimore. On each return the Flight Captain gathered the crew, the ground engineers, and anybody else who had been concerned in the voyage, to discuss its history in detail at a session called a flight survey. The limits of the subjects to discuss were usually of no greater note than slight mechanical improvements, often such details as the supply of sweet biscuits from America for the passengers.

But at one session there was matter enough – matter for congratulation.

Winston Churchill, in his siren suit, talking to Captain Shakespeare, Chief Officer of the Boeing flying-boat *Berwick*. It brought the Prime Minister back from Bermuda to Britain, in 18 hours non-stop, during the days of critical decision, early in 1942.

CHAPTER 19

Priority Passenger

IN THE EARLY days of 1942, Berwick was detained at Baltimore on official instruction. The Prime Minister, Mr. Winston Churchill, and the staff of his first mission to America, were at that time conferring with President Roosevelt in Washington.

News of the visit faded from the newspapers, and the new battleship, HMS Duke of York, vanished quietly from Chesapeake Bay; it was the general guess that the Prime Minister had sailed in her. But on January 12th the Flight Captain of Boeings, Captain J.C. Kelly Rogers, was called to the British Embassy in Washington where, under a seal of secrecy and with no names mentioned, he was told to prepare for a special flight to Bermuda. He was to be followed by two American Clippers to carry other members of a party of 90 passengers to be taken to that island.

Intricate devices were arranged to hide the fact that Berwick was engaged on anything unusual. All the routine of a normal Atlantic flight was undergone. The crew passed through Customs and Immigration, signals were made; but at the last moment the two pursers changed into civilian clothes and drove by car to Washington, where they boarded a special train and got to work preparing the luggage of the official party. Meanwhile Captain Kelly Rogers, with the rest of his crew, took off from Baltimore; not till they were airborne did the captain tell the crew that they were not proceeding direct to Bermuda, but to the harbour of Norfolk, Virginia, to pick up an important load of passengers.

The two Clippers moored up at Norfolk soon after Berwick, and the captains held conference in the Commanding Admiral's office at the air station. It was arranged that Berwick would lead the formation until they were one hour out from Bermuda. Then one of the Clippers, breaking wireless silence to obtain radio bearings from a ship stationed near Bermuda for that purpose, would take the lead.

The crew slept aboard Berwick and rose at 4 a.m. Half an hour later, when the special train arrived from Washington, the guessed-at secret of the identity of the official party was revealed; it was, of course, the Prime Minister and members of his mission. Mr. Churchill was the last to come aboard Berwick, full of interest at the size and comfort of the flying-boat. Soon after he was aboard she slipped the buoy and took off into a cloudless winter sky with light surface haze. She was carrying 25 of the party, distributed throughout her cabins. The Prime Minister was placed in the private cabin, the peacetime "honeymoon suite" in the tail. He took breakfast there, though every other meal on board he took in the saloon, with the rest of the party.

After breakfast, when he had changed into his famous siren suit, the Prime Minister was conducted round the flying-boat by Captain Rogers. He seemed impressed by her equipment and structure, and noted particularly the walkways inside the wings, into which an engineer can go to adjust the engines in flight.

As he reached their duty stations, the members of the crew were introduced to Mr. Churchill – Captain A.C. Loraine the co-pilot, Captain Shakespeare the chief officer, First Officer R.G. Buck the navigator, and the others. At this time Berwick was flying at 8,000 feet through a clear blue sky above a layer of cumulus cloud. Mr. Churchill, having been assured that it was perfectly safe to smoke, lit a cigar and eagerly accepted Captain Rogers's invitation to try Berwick's controls for himself. He took the captain's seat and flew her with enthusiasm for about 20 minutes, once putting her into a couple of slightly banked turns, and commenting on the vast differences between this flying-boat and the first aircraft he had flown in 1913.

They reached the point at which the American Clipper was to take the lead into Bermuda itself. Mr. Churchill listened to the brief conversation between Captain Rogers and the Clipper's pilot, Lieutenant Gillespie of the United States Navy. It seemed unwise for the Prime Minister to speak to Gillespie over the radio, but he was introduced to him at Bermuda next day.

When they reached Bermuda Mr. Churchill was invited to take the co-pilot's seat for alighting, which was made after a brief sight-seeing circuit of the island on January 15th.

Captain Rogers did not know, once he had alighted at Bermuda, whether anything more would be required of him. As he was lunching in Berwick on the harbour waters, however, a launch came out with a message that he was required immediately at Government House. There he was cordially greeted by the Prime Minister who said that they were going to have a conference, with himself in the chair; the other members of the conference included Air Chief Marshal Sir Charles Portal, Admiral of the Fleet Sir Dudley Pound, the Prime Minister's Flag Commander, his secretary Mr. Martin, and Captain Gordon Store of British Overseas Airways. It was held in the drawing-room of Government House, through the windows of which could be seen H.M.S. Duke of York riding at anchor in the harbour.

Mr. Churchill opened the conference. "Outside lies the Duke of York

Winston Churchill at the controls of the Boeing 314A Clipper G-AGCA, *Berwick.*

waiting to take me to England, which I can reach in seven to nine days," he said. "During that time I have ears to hear but no lips with which to speak. On the other hand, Captain Kelly Rogers assures me that in the aeroplane in which we have flown to Bermuda to-day we can fly to England to-morrow in not more than 22 hours. This is many days saved, and during that time many things may happen. Two important battles may be fought, and one major decision." He paused, and then added, "Such a flight cannot be regarded as a war necessity, but it is a war convenience."

The conference then resolved into a stringent cross-examination of Captain Rogers on the capabilities of his flying-boat, and of what his actions would be in various possible emergencies. Although naturally anxious that flight should be chosen, for the honour it would pay to the British merchant air service, the captain could not ignore the importance and responsibility of such a passenger; he tried to avoid giving the impression of seeking to influence the Prime Minister in his decision.

At last Mr. Churchill turned to the conference with the remark, "He seems to have all the answers, doesn't he?" Captain Rogers said that he felt confidence in speaking as he did, simply because the merchant airmen had gained sufficient experience to regard such a flight as an everyday occurrence, a result of "having all the answers." The Prime Minister decided that, should weather conditions permit a start the following morning, he would travel by air; should the forecast forbid the start that morning, he would go in the Duke of York. Sir Charles Portal would act for him in all matters relating to the flight, but the final decision as to whether to proceed would be taken by Captain Rogers. The passenger list would be restricted to seven, headed by the Prime Minister himself, Sir Charles Portal, Sir Dudley Pound and Lord Beaverbrook.

It can be imagined with what feelings the captain visited the meteorological offices that day, where, under the charge of Dr. Macky, the weather forecasts were being prepared. Captain Rogers admitted that he had thrown away the idea that the flight was a routine matter, finding himself with no wish to sleep, nor to eat much. He entered into calculations of fuel, deciding to take 5,000 U.S. gallons, making the all-up weight of the flying-boat 87,684 lb. at take-off. Similarly, each member of the crew was engaged in preparation in his own particular province.

Early next morning, January 16th, the two pilots and the navigator went to the meteorological office, where the final forecast was just being made. It showed considerable cloud over the English shore. They sent a signal to all stations concerned giving the estimated time of arrival at Pembroke Dock, in Britain, as 09.00 hours G.M.T. next morning, with a calculated flight time of 17 hours 25 minutes from take-off to touch-down.

By 10 o'clock in the morning the passengers came down to the quay, Mr. Churchill sunning himself on a veranda of the airport building, waiting for take-off. By 11.36 hours Berwick was slipping her moorings and taxying out. In spite of her load, she lifted from the water only 57 seconds after her throttles were opened. She climbed swiftly to 8,000 feet, to gain the most of the following wind, and settled down to cruising speed, on the rhumb line course from Bermuda to Pembroke Dock.

Perhaps one may be permitted a few intimate glances at this distinguished party of passengers, during the first transatlantic flight by a British Prime Minister, or for that matter by the leader of any nation. One may see them gathering at lunch in the saloon, talking of matters of State which had been concluded at Washington, the Prime Minister afterwards lighting his cigar and inviting the flying-boat's captain to join them at coffee, confessing to the sense of fun with which he was enjoying his journey, and the surprise with which his colleagues in England would find him amongst them five days before he was expected; then retiring to his private cabin to sleep for a little while, afterwards to open a brief-case, summon his secretary, and get to work.

Perhaps one may even watch the Chief of the Air Staff, relaxing with his fellow travellers through the long hours of flight, confounding the First Sea Lord with a few card tricks. And if that is something of an intrusion, surely one can follow Sir Charles Portal, Lord Beaverbrook and Sir Dudley Pound on to the flight deck, displaying great interest in the working of the flying-boat, and the processes of her navigation. Several times the captain was called to the private cabin where Mr. Churchill was working, to report on the progress of the flight; later he issued frequent bulletins, stating the aircraft's position, speed, fuel consumption, and so on.

After dinner, when darkness had fallen, Mr. Churchill and Lord Beaverbrook ascended to the flight deck, where they stood for some while gazing through the windows at the brilliantly starlit sky through which Berwick was riding, with Stardust brushed across the carpet of cloud below. In such serenity, they told Captain Rogers that they envied him his job. Later they flew into cloud, and ice began to form on the wings. The captain focused a spotlight on the leading edge of the wing, and asked them to watch the ice being broken off as he operated the "de-icer boots" – a mechanism which moves the leading edge with a wriggling motion, splitting away the ice.

Until darkness fell, and they could take a sight of the stars, the crew did not know how fast they had been travelling, for they were deliberately keeping wireless silence. They knew by the sun that they were on track, but the first star fix showed them to be 90 miles ahead of the flight plan, having averaged 199 miles an hour since take-off, and reached a speed of 207 miles during the last hour. The engines were running sweetly, with the carburettors on hot air for a great deal of the journey, as they flew through ice every time they touched rain or cloud.

In his own mind the captain was checking off, as they passed them, the various milestones in any long-distance ocean flight – the point of "three-engine non-return," the point of "four-engine non-return," the points at which various alternative alighting places such as the Azores or Gibraltar were eliminated from his plans (he always had enough fuel to alight at any alternative place in the British Isles). Towards dawn, when Mr. Churchill was dressing after a good sleep in his cabin, and putting on the shoes which the steward had insisted on warming to a nice temperature for him in the oven in his galley, the radio officers were gathering weather reports from Britain which spoke of deteriorating conditions.

At dawn, Mr. Churchill came up to the flight deck to watch the sunrise – that sunrise over the Atlantic which seen, from an aircraft is comparable to no other in the world. Beneath them the indeterminate floor of cloudtops was almost, black, the sky ahead dark grey. But then that sky was faintly tinged with the most delicate washes of pink and orange, while the floor clouds deepened to rich, full purple. The stalwart wings of Berwick, in grim black outline against this colour, seemed almost motionless in flight. Then the colours strengthened, the topmost tips of all the clouds below picked up a glow of pink on their eastern slopes, so that dotted over that whole floor of deep purple were small daubs of gleaming pink; till along the horizon came the fiery line that promises the sun himself, the outer circle of the propeller paths caught the glow, and the mystery of colours was lost in full day.

The captain had scant time to watch the dawn. Just as it broke he began his power descent from 10,000 feet, until 50 minutes later he was at only 1,000 feet, and approaching Land's End. The sky at this time was remarkably clear, and look-outs had been quietly posted through the aircraft against the approach of enemies. Mr. Churchill, indeed, did inquire casually what would be done were enemy aircraft to be sighted, but the captain practised his solitary moment of evasion, and managed to avoid without remark the one question he would rather not be asked.

In such a clear sky, he afterwards confessed, he was feeling a little too naked for comfort. But the weather soon changed to rain showers, and then fog. He had already learned that weather at Pembroke Dock was shutting down fast, with a visibility of only 500 yards, and had adopted the suggestion to change course towards Plymouth, where the clouds covered the sky at 1,000 feet, and visibility was four miles. Now, with fog, he asked on the radio for his first bearing, and then set course to pass just south of the Lizard. He had climbed to 1,500 feet, to fly just over the top of dense fog, beneath which, he told Mr. Churchill who was seated in the co-pilot's seat, lay the English coast.

Captain Shakespeare took that seat for the final approach, which was made on the automatic direction-finder; a few minutes later he said, "The coast." Looking down, Captain Rogers could see the Mewstone through the fog, then Statton Heights, then the RAF station at Mount Batten, his destination. As he circled the Sound, he noted that the balloon barrage had been short-hauled. On his first descent he lost horizontal visibility, so he climbed and circled again; this time, with Drake's Island just visible ahead but the Hoe shrouded, he crossed the breakwater at 50 feet, throttled back and alighted. Weather conditions had certainly been deteriorating, but the captain stated they had caused him "no concern whatsoever."

Thus the Prime Minister made his first Atlantic crossing, a journey of 3,365 statute miles from Bermuda to Plymouth, which had been flown in 17 hours 55 minutes. The flight time had been a little faster than anticipated, but the diversion to Plymouth at the end had added something to its length. Actually, having signalled from Bermuda an estimated time of arrival of 09.00 hours G.M.T., Berwick touched down at Plymouth at 08.59 hours on January 17th, one minute ahead of schedule.

While still on board, Mr. Churchill caused to be prepared a statement to the public, announcing his journey and the manner in which he had travelled, so that the world might be told he had been brought safely home by the British merchant air service. Next day Captain Rogers was invited to join a family reunion luncheon at No. 10 Downing Street, in order that Mrs. Churchill might express to him her thanks for having carried her husband safely back to her.

The announcement of that flight was of great value to the British merchant airmen, for only on such occasions were their services in the war fully realised by the public. The airmen were greatly proud of having been entrusted with the task. What was not so generally realised at the time was that, although the passengers made this a flight of outstanding importance and responsibility, the actual mechanism of it was a matter of routine. Many such long-distance flights had been made before by British merchant airmen, and many more have been made since; had that not been so, they could never have had the confidence to accept the task at all.

A few months later Mr. Churchill plainly demonstrated the confidence which he himself felt in the transatlantic services of the British airmen. In My 1942 he made the double journey, to America and back to Britain, in Bristol, one of the other Boeing flying-boats of British Overseas Airways. Captain Rogers was once more in command, with Captain Loraine as his second pilot, and Captain Shakespeare acting as chief officer. On the outward journey, in addition to the crew of 12, Bristol carried 10 passengers on a nonstop flight of 27 hours.

This double journey, longer and more tiring than the first, since a westbound crossing is much the harder of the two, also passed off with complete success. But it was no more than an emphasis of the lesson of the January flight – that the British merchant air service in wartime had proved itself so trusty as to be given the honour of carrying the leader of the nation over the Atlantic passenger route, a route which the airmen had created during and in spite of the war itself.

CHAPTER 20

Bombers to Britain

FLYING-BOATS WERE not the only aircraft which the British merchant airmen put on the Atlantic run during the course of the war. Notable as that service was, it had its roots in pre-war organisation and trials, and behind it lay the long experience of the men of Imperial Airways in the operation of flying-boats. But another service, later to be known as the North Atlantic Return Ferry, was created during the war from nothing: it had no reservoir of experience upon which to draw save that of the skilled airmanship of the captains and navigators, and the route over which an all-the-year-round service was maintained was declared by many experts to be impossible during the winter.

The British airmen proved in the air that it was possible to fly it in all weathers, and for the first two winters they were the only men in the world to keep up a two-way service over the North Atlantic. During the third winter they were joined on the route by the merchant air service of Canada.

Britain had one important advantage on this route. Just as at the eastern end of her Empire lines she could count on the co-operation of the vigorous and daring airmen of Australia, so at the western she was sure of help from those equally bold and enterprising men of Canada. The Canadians, indeed, proved their worth to the war, not only on the international routes, but inside their own country. And since it is to Canada that the story now crosses, here is the place to say something of what the Canadians achieved within the boundaries of that Dominion.

At the time there were two main air line organisations in Canada. Trans-Canada Air Lines, founded by Act of Parliament in 1937 as a State-owned air service, operates a trunk route across the Dominion from east to west, from Moncton, New Brunswick, to Vancouver, British Columbia, passing through the great cities of the country; a feeder line serves Calgary and Edmonton, Alberta. The Canadian Pacific Railway, which had meantime been acquiring the chief north-to-south privately-owned air lines of Canada, formed them in 1942 into the other big concern, Canadian Pacific Air Lines.

In brief, Trans-Canada Air Lines link eastern to western Canada, and Canadian Pacific Air Lines link northern to southern. Not only have these two air lines, throughout the war, concentrated on carrying over the regular routes mainly passengers vital to the war effort, or Government freight and mail, they have also made notable contributions on the ground by performing engineering work for the Royal Canadian Air Force, and by supplying training schools for the fighting airmen.

Similarly, on the ground the Civil Aviation Division of the Canadian Department of Transport has thrown itself whole-heartedly into the development of the Commonwealth Air Training Scheme, without which there would have been no swelling torrent of trained airmen to flow into the squadrons in Britain and the Middle East. To the Air Services Branch went the responsibility for finding sites for, and then constructing and equipping the numerous airfields that were required.

Besides all this, there were two projects in particular in which Canadian merchant airmen took a considerable share in the war.

In the summer of 1940 air transport was called upon to help build two large control dams, on Lake Manuan and on the Peribonca river, in the vast watersheds north of the mouth of the river Saguenay where it runs into the St. Lawrence west of Quebec. These dams were needed for the Shipshaw water-power project, power for the plant of the Aluminium Company of Canada, making the raw metal for the fighting aircraft of the war.

The airmen were asked to fly 4,000 tons of equipment and stores into a territory inaccessible to any other form of transport. They did it with nine aircraft, most of them veterans, of Canadian Airways (later a part of Canadian Pacific Air Lines), between August 1940 and October 1941. They carried out their ferry from Beauchene, on the eastern shore of Lake Onatchiway, due north along the Shipshaw and Manuan rivers to Lake Manuan. The aircraft operated on floats until the waters froze, then they switched over to skis; they went back to floats after the ice had broken up again.

The freight they carried varied from Diesel shovels and a sawmill, tractors and a motor-boat, dynamite and bulldozers, to six horses, four oxen and a cow. The largest aircraft they had was a Junkers 52. One of the horses, although roped, got his feet loose on the journey and added to the normal hazard of flying. The oxen travelled stoically, packed in with hay, most of which they ate on the way. The cow was kept asleep by an expert who travelled with her exerting slight pressure on her jugular vein.

They got 700 tons of assorted freight up to Manuan before the freeze of 1940; by April 1941 they had raised the total to nearly 2,000 tons, and they flew the whole 4,000 tons in by October. The record haul for one day was 29 tons by six aircraft in 24 round journeys.

The second area in which the merchant airmen particularly helped the war effort lay on the far side of the Dominion, in the north-west territories. For several years before the war young men had been pioneering the air above those vast, romantic, almost unpeopled northlands. Men of vision had seen in those skies the realisation of an age-long explorers' dream – the north-west passage to Asia.

A glance at a globe (not a flat map) will show how near lie the cities of Asia to those of the Americas, if the route taken leads through the north-western skies of Canada. Even without looking beyond the country's borders, there was new wealth to be sought and found; it was the first aircraft, piloted by one of the young pioneers, C.H. Dickins, to land at Great Bear Lake which carried the prospector Gilbert LaBine to the world's largest radium mine. Already by 1937 another pioneer, Grant McConachie, had opened up passenger and mail services from Edmonton in Alberta through the valley of the Liard, in northern British Columbia, to Whitehorse and Dawson in the Yukon. This route was afterwards pushed on to Fairbanks, in Alaska, 3 degrees south of the Arctic Circle.

This north-west airway opened up a country which had always defied river navigation of any practical quantity. It is not the desolate wasteland that has been imagined, but a succession of heavily timbered valleys under the rampart of the Rockies to the west, of great rivers such as the Athabaska, hurrying to the Arctic, of almost untouched stands of spruce, jack pine, poplar and birch. Some have spoken of it as the new Canada of the future. The Department of Transport firmly supported the efforts to open the skies of those territories to a modern air route, equipped with substantial airfields and the necessary radio aids to navigation. In 1939 a survey party was sent out and was in the field at the outbreak of war. The surveyors were not recalled; it was upon their survey that was based the construction of the North-West Airway, urged for the defence of Alaska by the Canada-United States Permanent Joint Board on Defence in 1940.

The Canadian Government undertook the main section, as far as the Yukon-Alaska border, at its own expense, constructing the airfields and the service roads, ferrying supplies by air, river and road, and setting up the radio stations. The story of the construction of this airway is in itself a little saga of endurance and pioneering; all that can be said here is that, by the end of 1941, the North-West Airway was open to through traffic, with airfields, radio stations, and permanent buildings at 200-mile intervals from Edmonton to Alaska. When Japan came into the war, Canada threw open to the United States an airway in working order, of immense assistance in transporting the forces which had to be hastened to the north to protect Alaska from a possible Japanese invasion. The air route in itself proved a powerful channel along which flowed American air reinforcements in great numbers. But it proved something even more. The United States undertook the construction of the famous Alaska Highway, the military road along which armies and supplies could be passed to ensure the safety of America's most northerly province.

That the Alaska Highway was built in the amazingly short space of six months was due to the skill of the American engineers; it was immeasurably assisted by the fact that Canada could offer them air service, fully equipped, along the whole route. Over that route flew the survey parties, the men pushing on to remote and otherwise inaccessible parts, and the supplies they needed. It is fitting that the Highway itself has now made the air route far easier to organise; that the two in combination have opened up vast new northern territories for the post-war years, and laid the foundations for the fastest air route from the Americas to the Far East.

It was to airmen of this calibre, therefore, that the British Ministry of Aircraft Production could look for help when, in the dark days of 1940, it was planned to ferry American-built bombers directly across the North Atlantic from Canada to reinforce the front-line squadrons of the hard-pressed RAF.

In the summer of that year the Canadian Pacific Railway agreed to organise the departure end in Canada. It set up an Air Services Department under the chairmanship of Sir Edward Beatty, G.B.E., with Mr. G.E. Woods-Humphery, formerly managing director of Imperial Airways, as his second in command. British Overseas Airways agreed to lend to this organisation, experts from its own staff to run the technical side. Captains A.S. Wilcockson, D.C.T. Bennett, R.H. Page and I.C. Ross, all senior captains of great experience – Wilcockson, for example, was the captain of the first transatlantic survey by Caledonia in 1937 – arrived in Canada at the beginning of August. Lieutenant-Colonel H. Burchall, formerly a senior official of British Overseas Airways, became general manager of the new organisation, and the captains took over the flying and operational side of it. They were soon joined by Squadron Leader (later Air Commodore) C.J. Powell, another Imperial Airways transatlantic captain who had entered the R.C.A.F.

Captain D.C.T. Bennett (later Air Vice-Marshal Bennett, leader of the RAF's Pathfinders), and Captain Page, went to the Lockheed aircraft factory in California, to take over the first two Hudson aircraft which were to be used as trainers for the transatlantic crews. It was a neutrality anomaly of those days that they had to return as passengers in the Hudsons which when they reached the Canadian border, had to be grounded and towed across by a horse before they could be flown to St. Hubert airfield, near Montreal, where the nucleus of the organisation had been set up.

A couple of months were spent in training, in modifying the first Hudson bombers delivered to Montreal to face the Atlantic, and in organising a small ground staff at St. Hubert airfield and at Gander airfield, formerly known as Hattie's Camp, in Newfoundland, whence the transatlantic flights were to start. This airfield stands at 400 feet above the level of Gander Lake, connected with the outside world on the surface only by a railway – there were no roads over the surrounding countryside of stunted trees, rivers, lakes and muskeg, a bog of rotting vegetation and water, presenting the most desolate appearance. The only buildings on the airfield were one hangar and one administration hut. For living accommodation, two railway sleeping coaches and a diner were shunted on to a siding.

The existence of this airfield in the wilds of Newfoundland was due to the combined work of the Civil Aviation Department of the British Air Ministry, the Newfoundland Government, and the hard work of Newfoundlanders in difficult circumstances. It was developed, as was the Shannon airport in Eire, as an outcome of the conference at Ottawa in 1935. It cost the British Government about £1,000,000, the Newfoundland Government paying one-sixth of the total cost, and sharing maintenance and operational costs, but when war came that sum was found a splendid investment, the value of Gander to the war effort far exceeding its original cost. The Canadian Government have undertaken operational responsibility since 1941 as a wartime measure.

The airmen at Gander, however, still lacked aircraft to deliver, in that summer of 1940, and crews with whom to deliver them. They also lacked the confidence of many outside air experts. It is essential to remember that transatlantic flying is basically a weather problem. The Atlantic had never before been flown in either direction in winter. Many experts said that, at the then stage of aviation development, it could not be done. Captain Bennett, on whom, as Flying Superintendent, fell the main burden of the actual operation, was determined to do it, not only with single aircraft but with formations. It is difficult to rate too highly the contribution which this captain made to the conquest of the Atlantic by land-planes. All of that small band of pioneers deserved well of their country and of the world in general; none of them would deny that Captain Bennett was at once the inspiration and the technical brain to which the success of the venture was primarily due.

The lack of men was remedied by the loan of 12 complete crews of British Overseas Airways, who sailed for Montreal in September 1940, and by recruiting Canadian and American individual airmen who were ready for the adventure. All the training was given by the most experienced of the British captains and radio officers. The lack of aircraft was remedied by the delivery, at intervals, of the first batches of Hudson bombers from the Lockheed factory.

Early in November the first six Hudsons were positioned on the airfield at Gander where snow was already piling high. The crews – three men to each aircraft – included English, United States, Canadian and Australian airmen. The plan was that Captain Bennett, in a seventh aircraft, should lead the other six in formation across the Atlantic to Aldergrove in Northern Ireland; he himself would do all the navigation, which the others would follow, by visual contact as long as possible, and by radio communication if they lost sight of him. He had prepared for each captain a copy of his flight plan, giving technical details for each section of the journey, and instructions on courses and heights to fly, engine settings, and such matters.

On November 10th, 1940, Captain Bennett took off in the seventh Hudson from Montreal for Gander, sending radio instructions as he flew that the whole formation was to be ready to leave that night. When he landed at Gander during the afternoon the snow and ice had been cleared away from the six other aircraft, and all was ready. Dinner awaited the crews in the dining coach, the band of the Queen's Own Rifles had arrived to play them off, and each man wore in his lapel a poppy made in Montreal for Remembrance Day – they had complete confidence that they would land in the British Isles on November 11th.

The band reassuringly played "There'll always be an England," as the crews climbed into their aircraft. As the motors roared, and they took off one by one, the airmen waved cheerfully to the band, which had struck up again (though one of them said his enthusiasm would have been damped had he known they were playing "Lead, kindly light"). The first Hudson, Captain Bennett, took off at 22.22 hours G.M.T., the others following quickly, and forming up over the airfield. Captain A. Andrews was follow-up man. When the formation was complete, it turned and set course to the east.

They flew at between 16,000 and 19,000 feet. For the first few hours the weather was clear at that height and they flew under the brilliance of a shining moon. As had been anticipated, however, one by one the aircraft lost sight of each other, but the regular radio instructions from the leading aircraft were sufficient for navigation. All were out of visual contact by the time they reached 20 degrees west of longitude, where awaited them a weather front through which they were to fly for the rest of the journey.

They were flying fast, with a tail-wind component of about 24 knots. But it was cold, the temperature ranging downwards to 22° C. Worst of all was the lack of oxygen. This was the one serious miscalculation of the flight. Each aircraft carried oxygen bottles containing only about 20 minutes' supply, which had to be sucked into the mouth through a primitive rubber tube. It was wildly insufficient. In some of the aircraft, men lost consciousness; some of the captains flew the latter half of the journey in a dreamy daze, doling themselves out sips of oxygen in just sufficient quantities to keep going. Lack of oxygen was particularly felt in one or two aircraft in which minor mechanical troubles developed – the fusing of a radio switchbox, a leak from an oil tank. Both engines of one aircraft cut for a moment when a fuel tank went dry earlier than had been expected, but picked up immediately when they were turned over to another tank.

At 08.50 hours G.M.T. next morning, November 11th, Captain Bennett touched down at Aldergrove. As he did so the second Hudson, piloted by Captain S.T.B. Cripps, a grey-haired veteran who took his wings in the 1914 war, and on this journey actually passed his 10,000th hour of flying, was circling the airfield. The first two of the seven, having flown the Atlantic, without visual contact during the latter part of the flight, had arrived at the destination within a few seconds of each other. Some minutes later the third aircraft, Captain R.E. Adams, landed beside them. Like most of the others, he had flown somewhat north of the course and made landfall among the islands. Captain Bennett took a stand at the window of the control tower at Aldergrove, watching. The whole future of the transatlantic ferry service depended on the next few minutes.

Within an hour from the first landing, all the rest came safely in. The flight was a complete success. The 22 airmen, wearing their Canadian poppies, went to an hotel for a meal and a shave. They pretended, for security reasons, that they had just flown in from England, though it is doubtful whether the receptionist, faced by this group of unshaven men, speaking in various accents of England, Canada and America, clad in anything from ten-gallon hats and Texan boots to Captain Bennett's invariable neat black homburg and brief-case, swallowed that story.

The airmen really did not care what was thought. They had done what experts had declared impossible. They had flown a formation of bombers to Britain across the North Atlantic in winter. They had cleared the course for that great stream of military aircraft of all kinds which was to flow over the ocean in swelling numbers as the war proceeded. They had given the first proof that, in the post-war years, a daily air service between the Americas and Britain was no longer a dream.

When they had flown their aircraft on to England, the airmen were immediately put into a ship to return to Canada for future flights.

The second formation flight of seven Hudsons, led by Captain Page, left Gander on November 29th, arriving safely in the British Isles the following morning. Captain A.G. Store led the third group flight of seven Hudsons during the night of December 17th-18th. Captain Bennett brought the fourth group flight across on December 28th-29th, although only four aircraft reached Britain; one of the others crashed on take-off, without injury to the crew, the wreck on the runway at Gander preventing a second from starting at all, while a third had to turn back with engine trouble.

Formation flights were then abandoned. The difficulties of keeping contact in actual practice had proved extreme, and more navigation instruments and trained navigators were becoming available. Henceforward, all the flights were made singly, each aircraft taking off from Gander and proceeding as it became ready.

From these beginnings, the ferry-delivery of bombers to Britain was speedily strengthened. More buildings were put up at Gander with "East-bound Inn" replacing the railway sleepers and dining-coach. St. Hubert airfield, proving less than satisfactory for the heavier aircraft, was to be abandoned in favour of Dorval, a large airfield some miles from the outskirts of Montreal, close to the French-Canadian villages with their villas, sailing craft, and silvered church spires, that stand among the pines and maples of the shore of Lake St. Louis. Over the Atlantic itself Captain Bennett made in secrecy an aerial photographic-survey of Greenland, mapping an alternative route to the north. In Montreal, there were changes in organisation. The first RAF crews began to arrive in Canada for the delivery flights.

As a matter of policy, the transatlantic ferrying of bombers became a matter for Governmental organisation; that does not in the least detract from splendid services performed by the Canadian Pacific Railway Company in launching and organising the Atlantic ferry in the early days.

From March 1941 onwards, control was gradually being taken over by the Atlantic Ferry Organisation – with a short title of Atfero – of the British Ministry of Aircraft Production, working in close collaboration with the Governments of the United States and Canada; the Canadian Pacific control was not officially ended until July 15th, and many of the key personnel of that company continued to serve under Atfero.

On July 20th Atfero formally passed into the control of Ferry Command of the RAF, under Air Chief Marshal Sir Frederick Bowhill. Two years later, on the formation of RAF Transport Command under the same officer, the Atlantic Ferry became No. 45 (Atlantic Transport) Group of that Command.

Chapter 21

On Top of the Weather

IT WILL BE recalled that when they delivered the first seven Hudsons from Newfoundland to Britain, the crews were at once placed in a ship and taken back to Canada for a further flight. Surface shipping was then the only transport available to get them back. Yet it was obviously undesirable to ferry bombers across the Atlantic at, say, 200 miles an hour, only to be compelled to send the crews back for more in a ship travelling at 10 knots. Air crews' flying time was a precious commodity in those days.

The solution was to organise a two-way air service by land-plane across the North Atlantic. Now this was a formidable undertaking, for to be of any real value such a service would have to operate with considerable regularity, winter and summer alike. Westbound crossings were always more difficult than eastbound, since the prevailing Atlantic winds were west winds; and less than 12 months before, even eastbound crossings had been considered by many impossible in winter.

Transport aircraft which could be expected to tackle a two-way Atlantic ferry of this kind did not then exist anywhere in the world. Seven military

Blanketed in snow, her propellers wrapped in protective stockings, a Liberator stands hull deep in the winter drifts of Dorval. Trenches have been cut and the foreground has been cleared by blower; an hour later she was airborne to Britain.

aircraft, Consolidated Liberator bombers, LB.30As and Bs, were therefore flown to Montreal and adapted for the attempt. The earlier of them were ready by late April 1941, and on May 4th the first eastbound and westbound flights were made simultaneously, between St. Hubert airfield at Montreal and Squire's Gate airfield near Blackpool, Lancashire.

Captain Bennett flew eastbound in a Liberator bearing the registration AM.258, and the manufacturer's serial number one; it was to become famous over the Atlantic. He carried four passengers, including Air Chief Marshal Sir Hugh Dowding, and 200 lb. of diplomatic mail, and made the flight, with a stop at Gander, in a total flying time of 14 hours 30 minutes.

Captain A.B.H. Youell, who piloted the westbound Liberator, was delayed at the start by an air raid on the Blackpool area during which a 1,000 lb. bomb exploded only 25 yards from his aircraft. Fortunately, the bomb, falling in sandy ground, did such slight damage that the Liberator was delayed for only 24 hours. Bad weather delayed him again for several days at Gander, but by May 9th he reached St. Hubert, after a total airborne time of only 16 hours 44 minutes, with seven passengers, all of them air crew returning to ferry more bombers to Britain. The first westbound Liberator had certainly been delayed, but it had swept the path for future flights. They followed rapidly.

In the next two months there were more than 20 flights in each direction; 128 passengers, 22,151 lb. of freight and 9,598 lb. of mail had been carried from Canada to Britain; 282 airmen returning for more bombers to ferry, 32 diplomatic passengers, 1,919 lb. of freight and 869 lb. of mail had been flown from Britain to Canada. Owing to bad weather conditions in Newfoundland, more than half of the westbound flights, the more difficult, had been forced to go direct from Britain to Montreal nonstop, a distance of 3,150 miles.

The two-way transatlantic ferry service had been firmly established with land-planes, at least during the summer months. The real test still lay ahead, in the ice, snow and gales of winter. Before that period was reached, the whole organisation of the return ferry was drastically changed. The air over the North Atlantic had taken on its wartime pattern. It had been realised that the delivery of bombers eastbound was properly the function of the RAF, and this responsibility was assumed by Ferry Command. It had equally been realised that the flying of a two-way passenger service, with the prime purpose of getting the ferry crews back to Canada, was properly a function of the merchant air service, with its long experience of flying to a schedule, and of the extra precautions of peacetime aviation.

Early in September, therefore, the North Atlantic Return Ferry was handed over completely to British Overseas Airways. Ten Liberator aircraft were provided by the RAF, but British Overseas Airways took full responsibility for their maintenance, their operation, and the provision of their crews. The Return Ferry was to be operated to the requirements of the Air Officer Commanding, Ferry Command; its only passengers were to be ferry crews returning from Britain, or men whom the Government wished to travel on war duties in either direction, and its cargoes would all be official freight and mail. But in every other respect it was to be a merchant air route. The first crossing under this new control was made eastbound on September 24th by Captain O.P. Jones, one of the veterans of the air, whose trim stature and pointed beard were widely known before the war by travellers in Europe.

British Overseas Airways then prepared to face the test of operating the first regular two-way transatlantic passenger services in winter. They were given a clear field. Merchantmen of other countries had flown the route during the summer months, but when snow and ice came down they removed their services to the south, and left the North Atlantic to the British Islanders.

They had the advantage of well-experienced meteorologists. At the western end they had the man who knew more, probably, about North Atlantic weather than any other, Mr. P.D. McTaggart-Cowan, who had been living in Newfoundland studying that subject since the pre-war preparations for transatlantic flights; none of the captains would grudge a tribute to the contribution this man has made to Atlantic flying. At the eastern end the equally long-experienced meteorologists had been moved from Foynes, where Eire's neutrality precluded the dissemination of secret information, to Gloucester, and were shortly to be moved to the airfield at Prestwick, on the Ayrshire coast of Scotland, which became the busy wartime terminal for the Atlantic air crossings.

Prestwick had first been "discovered" as a good Atlantic terminus by Captain E.P.M. Eves, who later lost his life on Atlantic service. In the quite early days he found he could put down there when bad weather hindered him from landing at the other airfields available. He walked across to the duty pilot's office to report, and, answering routine questions in the usual way, said he had come from Gander after a flight of 10 hours 54 minutes. "That seems a long flight," remarked the duty pilot. "I say, where have you come from? I'm not very sure where this place Gander is." Then it dawned on him that the captain before him had just flown the Atlantic. Other captains later noticed the good weather for landing at Prestwick, and, for this and other reasons, the eastern terminal was officially transferred to that airfield.

British Overseas Airways had one other big advantage on the ground, the long experience of their own and of Canadian airways engineers – much of the servicing in Canada was carried out by Trans-Canada Air Lines. The mechanical difficulties which the engineers had to overcome for that first winter of two-way flying were formidable. Most of them were problems of cold.

It should be understood that the first enemy of the airmen during the winter was ice. In any cloud between the temperatures of +2° and -18° C, sufficient clear ice is liable to form on the wings and hull of an aircraft to bring it down within two minutes. Captain G.R. Buxton, one of the original Atlantic Liberator pilots, had a fearful experience of that. Flying westbound, and incidentally with Beurling, an outstanding RAF Canadian fighter pilot of Malta as one of his passengers, his aircraft became coated with hard clear ice at a height of 18,000 feet. It came down, the pilot quite helpless, in a series of flat stalls to about 12,000 feet; it could not maintain greater height, and even then could struggle along at an air speed of only 100 miles an hour.

The flight plan envisaged a 12-hour journey to Gander, against strong headwinds. Unless he could increase his speed, Buxton knew he would never make it; if, on the other hand, he turned back, he knew he would have to fly once more through ice clouds that might bring him down into the sea. He decided to continue. He contrived to break the ice from the leading edges of the wings by operating the de-icer boots, and put the aircraft into a long, slow climb, eventually regaining height and most of his air speed. But when he reached Gander the ice was still packed behind the boots on the wings, and in all the outside crevices of the hull.

Ice, then, was the enemy to be avoided at all costs. The only safe methods were to fly over it or under it. Since, in winter, the freezing level over the Atlantic is often synonymous with sea level, to fly under the ice-clouds was impossible. The airmen therefore flew over them. At a height of 20,000 feet or more they found that the outside temperatures were less than -18° C.; more often than not they were between -40° and -50°. At such heights of coldness, there is insufficient moisture to form the dangerous clear ice. Only rime ice will form, and that can easily be dislodged, or disregarded. The secret of winter flying of the Atlantic, therefore, was to fly at 20,000 feet or more, above the ice-clouds. But the aircraft still had to rise and descend at each end. So mechanical devices, such as alcohol sprays inside the engines, and along the edges of the propellers, had to be fitted to the Liberators.

There still remained the problem of heating the interiors of the aircraft. The toughest airman faces unhappily a 10- or 12-hour flight in a temperature of -40°. For the passengers, some of them middle-aged men unaccustomed to flying, the prospect was severe. Several expedients were tried in turn to heat the cabins. The first was a heater (with two flames) in the tail, but the captains were so worried by it that they preferred to endure the cold rather than use it. Then heaters were installed working from donkey engines; but

Bearded with ice, a Boston bomber stands on the airfield at Gander. More perilous in the air, ice like this can drag a plane into the sea in a few minutes. The airmen flew over the ice-clouds; heaters cleared the aircraft during ascent and descent.

the engines spluttered out at heights greater than 10,000 feet. The heaters were then connected to the blower system of the aircraft engines; this time the return pipes were found to carry water that froze and lowered the engine boost. Finally, the heaters were connected to the engine's exhaust system, and the exhaust was dumped overboard. This proved to be the solution.

All this took a long time, and the earlier flights were made in severe discomfort. Since there were in those days no seats in the aircraft, the passengers lay muffled on mattresses on the floor. If a man dozed on the way over, or so much as removed his gloves, he was liable to severe frostbite. One passenger on a westbound journey thus lost all the fingers of both his hands.

Even when all possible precautions had been taken, there was still the hazard of accident. Captain L.V. Messenger, who was the first man to complete 50 Atlantic crossings, in the course of which he carried more than 1,000 passengers, owed his coldest flight to a seagull. Just after he had become airborne at Gander on a winter day, he collided with the gull. It smashed through the side blister of the cockpit, striking Messenger's face and covering him with its blood and entrails. What mattered, though, was that the bird had made a hole in the window a foot or more across.

The Liberators took off from Gander with such heavy loads of petrol that they could not put back immediately on to that airfield; the surface would not support them. The petrol could not be jettisoned, so that if the aircraft wished to turn back from aft Atlantic crossing, it had to circle Newfoundland for about four hours, ridding itself of the weight of fuel before it could land. Rather than do that, Messenger continued the flight to Britain, with wind of a temperature of -40° streaming through the broken window by the side of his head. In all his long years of flying he had never experienced such intense cold.

One aircraft, during this first winter, was compelled to essay the long consumption of fuel before putting down again at Gander. This Liberator took off on the night of November 7th-8th, 1941, with Captain O.P. Jones in command, and Captain A. Andrews as co-pilot.

Owing to a mechanical fault, they could not get the undercarriage to retract fully; the extra drag which this entailed forbade on that occasion an Atlantic crossing, and there was no option but to fly around Newfoundland until sufficient petrol had been consumed for them to land. To make matters worse, for a long time they could not persuade the undercarriage to return to the fully down position, and they flew with it half-extended, although at last they forced it down.

The trouble was that, while they were flying round the airfield on which they dared not land until so much petrol had gone, the weather was steadily closing in on the ground. The meteorologists had warned them when they took off that they had three hours in which to get clear of Newfoundland, after which weather over the island would have shut right in. Grimly, hour after hour, they circled the airfield just below the cloud base, getting lower and lower as the clouds descended.

When things were looking very bad, Captain Jones turned to his navigator with the remark, "All we need now to make us perfectly happy is to get thoroughly iced up." Ten minutes later it happened. A shower of freezing rain coated the windscreen with half an inch of ice. In order to be able to see at all, the co-pilot had to open a side window, put an arm out, and chip the ice from outside with a jack-knife.

Meanwhile the rest of the crew were having considerable trouble. In the effort to lower the undercarriage again all the hydraulic fluid was lost. Flight Engineer V. Stack collected coffee, lemonade, and other hot drinks on board the aircraft, and poured them into the hydraulics reservoir, two other members of the crew being put to the hand-pump – one of them murmuring dismally, "I never did like damned aeroplanes, anyway," and the other, "Shut up, you idiot, and pump."

After circling for three hours and five minutes, Captain Jones decided that he had got rid of sufficient fuel to risk a landing. It was the risk of desperation in any case, since the weather was almost down to the surface of the airfield, where an anxious crowd stood watching the Liberator; in another few moments a landing would be impossible. He made his last circuit and, with great skill and complete unconcern, put the still overladen aircraft down on the runway with practically no damage.

It was not to be expected that a captain of such long experience should be perturbed, even by such a dilemma as this; certainly not Captain Jones, to whom is credited the remark which must always rank as a classic of the Atlantic air. Midway across on one occasion the light at the instrument panel failed. The second pilot, making his first Atlantic flight, was at the controls at the time, and Captain Jones retired to the engineer's position, to write up his logbook by the glow from the dials on that panel. Flight Engineer Stack made way for him, and sat down on the floor to eat an apple.

At that moment, over the middle of the Atlantic, all four engines cut out simultaneously. It transpired later that the pilot, adjusting the automatic controls in darkness, had accidentally pulled the master switch for all engines. They were then at about 14,000 feet, and they glided rapidly to 6,000 feet before the captain, striding forward, had remedied the mishap and brought the engines to life again. But before he did so, he closed his logbook with some deliberation, laid his pen down beside it, turned to the engineer, and remarked, "Strangely quiet, isn't it, Mr. Stack?"

Captain Percy, another of the original Atlantic Liberator pilots, flew one night into cold so intense that his automatic pilot froze. His windscreen was completely ice-coated, and as he did not fancy flying the Atlantic manually by instruments, he tugged at a side window to open it and get some sort of horizon to guide him. The window opened with a jerk, and his oxygen mask, torn from his face, was precipitated through the window. Since he was flying at 20,000 feet, he immediately felt the effects of lack of oxygen. He put the aircraft hastily into a dive, when suddenly he heard something flapping about outside; it was the remains of his mask, torn to shreds, but still attached to the tube. He hauled it in, gripped it between his teeth, found that he could still suck the oxygen through, and came across the Atlantic in that manner, the only ill-effect an aching jaw.

Through many hardships and dangers the British airmen maintained the two-way North Atlantic service throughout the winter of 1941-42, and emerged, still flying, into the easier days of spring and summer. They had done what had been thought impossible, and they alone of all the airmen of the world had done it.

All the time improvements were being made – mechanical improvements to combat the weather; improvements in comfort, such as the placing of seats in the cabins for passengers. It was found that 14 seats could be placed inside each Liberator, though somewhat close together, when its interior had been reconstructed. That left the bomb bays, into which special racks were fitted, to carry freight.

Flights of note were continually being made. This does not mean flights in record time; such flights have no more meaning than curiosities. The job of the Atlantic captains is to bring their aircraft across the ocean in the safest, most economical manner, not to indulge in races. They pay so little attention to fastest speeds that one captain who had in fact broken the east-bound record was unaware of the fact, and even when he heard it announced some hours later in the BBC news, still did not realise that the item referred to him.

There are many things besides speed which make individual flights notable. Captain Cripps, the oldest man by 10 years in the Atlantic service, made several such. Just before starting westbound late one Saturday night he bought a copy of a British Sunday newspaper, dated for the following morning. Flying north of a depression he picked up a following wind, and arrived at Montreal at 6.4 a.m. local time. The newsvendor to whom he handed his British newspaper as a curiosity at 7 o'clock was amazed to find that it bore that same day's date.

On another occasion, flying in Liberator AM920, another famous Atlantic aircraft, he breakfasted in Scotland (though at 5 o'clock in the morning, rather early), and was at Dorval, Montreal, just in time for a late lunch at 2.30 in the afternoon, local time. His actual flying time on this non-stop journey was 13 hours 38 minutes.

To Captain Cripps also goes the distinction, if such it be, of carrying, so far as he is aware, the first stowaway on an Atlantic aircraft. He was a Canadian ground-engineer at Gander, who was most anxious to come to Britain to join up in the RAF. He simply walked aboard just before take-off, sat quietly in one corner, and nobody noticed him. In fact, nobody would have noticed him at all, had the crew not been warned of his presence by radio from Gander when they were two hours out. When they arrived, he was handed over to the guard-room at Prestwick.

The winter of 1942-43, the second in which the two-way crossings were maintained, proved even more testing than the first. Difficulties of cold and ice had been largely overcome, but during this winter the west winds blew with exceptional strength. These winds were of assistance, of course, to eastbound flights; so much so that, in February 1943, the ground speed averaged over 10 such flights was 270 miles an hour. Aircraft were flying on tailwinds of as high as 87 knots, and one flight was made with a tailwind of 93 knots.

But westbound was a different story. The captains flew whenever there was a reasonable prospect of being able to make sufficient speed against the wind to reach the other end. They completed westbound crossings against winds of 57, 58 and even on one occasion 70 knots. At higher velocities they could not make the attempt, and there was a short period during the winter when aircraft were accumulating in Britain, waiting for the wind to lessen in order that they might slip across.

The weather men had been advocating for some time, as a cure for these conditions, re-routing the westbound flights northabout through Iceland. In this way, there was every prospect of passing north of the main Atlantic depressions, and of picking up east winds beyond their circumference. The captains, however, were at first somewhat reluctant to try this method, until Captain W.S. May went off by the northern route and reached Canada while the others were still waiting at Prestwick. This trial flight gave the necessary confidence in the northern route, and soon it was considered the natural alternative when weather on the direct route was unfavourable. Thus, even at the height of winter, far better regularity was maintained.

In spite of these weather delays, which were confined to a short period and were not unduly lengthy, the British airmen maintained the two-way Atlantic service throughout its second winter. Once more the British civil air ensign was the only flag on regular service on the return route.

By that time they could fairly claim that they had conquered the North Atlantic air. Their knowledge of the route was such that they could perform with confidence crossings which, earlier, could not have been contemplated.

On August 23rd, 1943, for example, Captain Ben Prowse burst a tyre as he took his Liberator off from Gander, with the result that his undercarriage was jammed with one leg up, one down. He was carrying 12 passengers, freight, and a full petrol load, so immediate return to Gander was impossible. Since he knew that he would have to attempt a belly-landing wherever he put down, Captain Prowse considered he might as well do it in Scotland as in Newfoundland. He therefore turned east, and flew the Atlantic with the knowledge of the ordeal waiting for him at the other end.

Ambulances, fire-fighting kit and rescue parties were all standing-by at Heathfield in Scotland, when he arrived, on schedule. He made a belly-landing in a field close to the airfield. Nobody was hurt, the freight was undamaged, and only the propellers of the Liberator were bent. The Air Council commanded a letter be sent to Captain Prowse complimenting him on this "hazardous feat, at the end of a long flight, calling for presence of mind and airmanship of the highest order."

Another remarkable flight, in the opposite direction, was made by Captain W.L. Stewart. He was told at Prestwick that the Government urgently wanted to get to the De Havilland factory at Toronto some spare parts which were holding up the production of Mosquito aircraft which had been undertaken in Canada. He determined to fly them from Scotland to Toronto, overflying Montreal. The spares left London by train at midnight on a Sunday in September, arriving at Prestwick early on Monday afternoon. They were loaded into the Liberator, and on their way by teatime. Stewart refuelled at Reykjavik in Iceland, then flew direct to Toronto, which he reached early on Tuesday morning. By 8 o'clock in the morning, local time, on Tuesday, the spares were in the Toronto factory, actually being fitted on to the Mosquito aircraft, and production was flowing again. In December 1944 Captain Stewart was the first British pilot to complete one hundred Atlantic crossings.

It was during the summer of 1943 that Canada came on to the two-way Atlantic route, mainly for the purpose of carrying swift mail between the Dominion and her troops in Britain. Trans-Canada Air Lines, operating on behalf of the Canadian Government, adapted a Lancaster bomber for the route; the Canadian captains travelled a few times with those of British Overseas Airways to gain experience, and soon were working the route on their own. They carried passengers as well as mail, and took so readily to the route that within a few weeks Captain R.F. George, with Captain A. Rankin as co-pilot, put up a then record time of 12 hours 51 minutes from Montreal to Scotland. The Canadians continued on the route during the winter of 1943-44, so that there were two British merchant flags on regular, two-way service over the North Atlantic in that third winter of its operation.

Nobody making the land-plane journey now would realise that only such a short time has elapsed since the dangers and difficulties of the pioneer flights. It is possible now to sit of an evening on the wide balcony of the airport buildings at Prestwick, watching transport after transport slip down the wide runway and take off for Canada without any more fuss than an express train leaving London for Scotland; and to watch, in the early light of the morning, an equal number of aircraft put quietly down on the runway after a night-flight from the other side, crews and passengers who lunched at Montreal stepping out to take breakfast in the bright airport restaurant at Prestwick.

Behind the scenes the atmosphere is similarly that of commonplace routine. Before taking off, the captains and crews stroll to a large house of Victorian pattern overlooking the nearby golf-links, the only things to distinguish it from any other well-tended private residence a few radio masts among the flowerbeds, and in the front porch a small plaque bearing the words, "Transatlantic Air Control," with the emblem of a bird in flight

'Flight Plan'. BOAC navigation officers plan an Atlantic crossing. They are in the control room at Prestwick, terminus of the busy 3,000-mile trans-ocean traffic route.

beneath a crown. There, on the panelled walls of what was once the drawing-room, or perhaps the library, they study the charts and control blackboards of the Atlantic air, and talk to the controllers who, from their desks, will be in constant touch with them from the first moment of their flight.

There, in what was once perhaps the dining-room, now peopled by WAAF clerks and Air Ministry meteorologists, they study the weather reports, receive their briefings and their flight forecasts, determine which course to fly on the principle of one captain's remark that he might get his passengers a bit cold, but thanks to weather forecasts, he never got them wet. And when these vital preliminaries have been undertaken, the aircraft taxies round to the strip of concrete beneath the balcony of the airport building, baggage is wheeled out and placed aboard, the passengers put down their teacups in the café and take their seats, and one more Atlantic flight begins. Nowadays it is as much routine as that. Already from the balcony at Prestwick one can survey the picture of the daily Atlantic air service of the future.

Part VII

'THEY HAVE DESERVED WELL'

Captain Gilbert Rae, a BOAC Mosquito pilot. Rae was killed on 19 August 1944 when the Mosquito he was flying, G-AGKP, crashed into the North Sea five miles off the Scottish coast near Leuchers. At the time he was returning from Stockholm. The two other men on board, 2nd Radio Officer Donald Trevor Roberts and Captain Bernard William Basil Orton, the passenger, were also killed.

CHAPTER 22

High Road to Sweden

WHEN, IN THE early summer of 1943, the enemies were cleared from Africa, when the Red Army was making its gigantic strides towards the west, when the British-United States air assault on Germany and Occupied Europe was mounting from the British Isles, when Mr. Churchill could speak of "the end of the beginning," there seemed to be a signal for the United Nations to think of all matters in terms of building-up, of a happier future. Air transport was no exception. Men's minds turned, perhaps too precipitately, to contemplation of and argument about the tremendous part the air would play in a world at peace. There was planning of the merchant aircraft of the future, some strengthening of existing fleets; old routes were expanded, new pushed forward.

Before these are described it is necessary to turn back to the contemplation of one route which British airmen have maintained throughout the war, one of the most hazardous routes they have been called upon to fly, of the existence of which for a long while nothing was said.

Only a short time before the outbreak of war British Airways Ltd., one of the components to form British Overseas Airways, had started a weekly service between the British Isles, Norway, Sweden and Finland. It was the only European air service from Britain, apart from that to Paris, to continue after war began. It was one of the first routes to feel the impact of actual hostilities, for when war broke out between Finland and Russia, it had to be stopped at Stockholm. Before the route was thus curtailed, the aircraft evacuated many British subjects from Finland, and they continued to take Red Cross medical supplies to that country.

The service continued until April 1940, with Junkers Ju 52 and Lockheed 14 aircraft. But the aircraft that was preparing on an airfield at Perth to leave for Stockholm on April 9th was suddenly cancelled. On that morning, the German invasion had flooded into Norway and Denmark. Two of the Ju 52 aircraft were caught at the wrong end of the run, Jason at Oslo and Juno at Stockholm. Jason had to be abandoned to the Germans, but her crew managed to escape overland into Sweden and to come home a week later in Juno. The Airways traffic officer at Stavanger was missing for a few days, but later he turned up in England, having escaped from Norway and made his way across the North Sea in a fishing craft.

With Norway in the hands of the enemy, the airmen might well have been

181

excused for thinking the Scandinavian route no longer practical; indeed, for a time no regular service could be operated, and before the end of the year only nine special flights had been made direct from Perth to Stockholm. Yet the need for a regular service to Sweden was clear.

That country, soon to be the only remaining neutral in northern Europe, was completely surrounded by Axis troops. The only method of communication she still retained with Britain – with the whole outside world, for that matter – was the cable. Unless Britain's influence in Sweden were to be wholly surrendered to the enemy, it was vital to have some means of personal communication with that country; it could only be by air.

Only by air could she get into Sweden newspapers and magazines to do something to correct the Nazi propaganda with which the country was being drenched. Only by air could she send diplomats and other Government officials, to assert in Sweden the fact that Britain still fought the war, and intended to win it. Moreover, there was a very practical reason for desiring some sort of transport link. Every mechanical instrument of war must contain, in some part of its body, ball-bearings; they are as vital to mechanised war as guns or ammunition. Some of the finest ball-bearings of the world are produced in Sweden, and not only did Britain need to acquire them, she needed by doing so to prevent the enemy's having them. Early in 1941, therefore, British Overseas Airways was asked to recommence a regular service between Scotland and Stockholm.

Consider for a moment the magnitude of that request. Even though the aircraft flew at night, they had to fly, quite unarmed, directly over the waters of the Skagerrak, flanked on either side by some of Germany's most powerful anti-aircraft defences, within easy range of the enemy's radio detecting-devices and fighter squadrons. There were no air crews on this route who were not soon accustomed to searchlights and flak; and at those northern latitudes, even at night, they flew, sometimes in moonlight, or through skies lit by the crescendo and decrescendo of the Northern Lights. In summer there was scarcely any darkness at all.

The service was started "on a shoestring." The entire staff consisted of three members of the air crew, a traffic officer, an engineer, and a motor transport driver. There was only one aircraft, a Lockheed which Polish airmen had managed to bring to this country from their own when war began. As the identification letters of this stalwart were BG, it was known throughout the route as "Bashful Gertie, the Terror of the Skagerrak." After some months' service, Gertie blew an engine at Bromma, in Sweden, and had to remain there for a while. But the RAF released some Hudson aircraft to take its place, and the route continued to be flown. The fact that it was flown at all did much to persuade the Swedes that Britain might not, after all, be beaten.

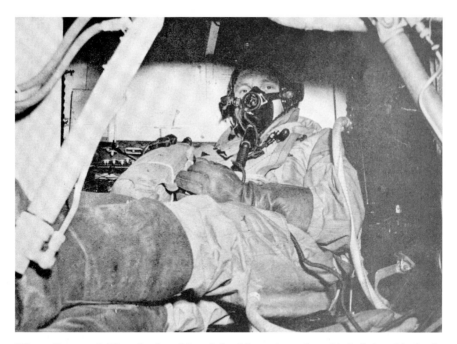

'Close Quarters'. The single cabin of the Mosquito – fast, high-flying blockade runner to Sweden – had no room for passengers. They were strapped down instead in the felt-lined bomb-bay, given a flask of coffee, and told to hope for the best.

When the airmen first arrived in Stockholm they were far from welcomed. Nobody said much to them, nobody would be seen about with them. But as the captains continued to arrive and depart with cheerful regularity, the atmosphere began to change. Cordiality is thought to have been given a fillip by one of the captains who, taking off just as an important-looking German aircraft arrived on the airfield at Bromma, Stockholm, contrived by an awkward lurch on the runway to smother completely in dust the august German general commanding all the Luftwaffe in Norway, Finland and Northern Europe. It was not long before the captains arriving at Stockholm arrived among friends.

The Scandinavian route had to be flown high, to minimise the danger of enemy fighters, and crew and passengers alike needed oxygen. Yet in the early days, one of the first passengers to be brought to England was the three and three-quarters-months-old baby of the Polish minister to Sweden. He travelled with great unconcern, emitting his first howl on arrival in Scotland. Leuchars was ultimately chosen as the Scottish terminal for the Scandinavian route, and as time went on the fleet of aircraft was reinforced. Some more Hudsons and some Lodestars were added, the latter being flown by Norwegian crews appointed by the Norwegian Government.

For a time in 1943 the Norwegians did most of the flying, but the British airmen were put back on the route to fly the Whitley bombers, converted into freighters, which had not proved a success on the Malta or West Africa routes, but which were the only aircraft available at that time. They proved equally unsuccessful to Scandinavia, nor was it pleasant for the crews to traverse the enemy defences of the Skagerrak at night in aircraft which, at that overload and thus converted, could not fly should one engine fail. After a time the Whitleys were discontinued.

In spite of the dangers of the route, the first mishap was not due to enemy action, but to mechanical failure which forced the Lodestar aircraft *Loch Leven* to turn back from over the Skagerrak and make a descent on to the sea off the Swedish coast. The captain, who was later lost in a Hudson which simply disappeared while returning from Stockholm, managed on this occasion to get all his passengers and crew into rubber dinghies and row them safely ashore.

It was a route that inevitably took toll of the men who flew it. Captain L.A. Wilkins, a man in his middle years, the pilot who probably did more than any other to establish the route and keep it flying regularly in spite of all the enemy arms that lay athwart it, also gave his life to it in the end. Yet the service was flown with such vigour that on some nights there were up to a dozen aircraft plying over the Skagerrak to and from Sweden at the same time.

After the failure of the Whitleys, other aircraft were proposed for Scandinavia. The C.W.20 Saint Louis made a few flights, and some slow Dakotas which were put on to the route shifted most useful loads. But in the summer of 1943 came a revolutionary change. The merchant airmen were provided with Mosquitoes, those military aircraft which the RAF made famous as then the fastest, as fighters or bombers, in the world. A few of the bomber type were converted for transport use. Since they are small aircraft, with room in the cabin only for a crew of two men, they can carry nothing bulky. But on this particular route they were needed to take only diplomatic mail, newspapers and magazines to Sweden, and to bring home ball-bearings. For that they were ideal. Their bomb-bays were fitted with baskets and hooks, so that they could be filled to cubic capacity with the ball-bearings, a cargo of great weight in little room.

The Mosquitoes were so fast that it was decided to let them attempt the flights to Stockholm in daylight. This seemed particularly to pique the Germans, that unarmed aircraft, of no matter how modern a design, should be able to traverse the coastal defences of their home waters, skirting Jutland itself in broad daylight. They went to considerable lengths to interrupt this route, moving fighter squadrons to its shores for that purpose.

Arguably, BOAC's most famous wartime route was the 'Ball-Bearing' run from Leuchars to Stockholm (Bromma), using, initially, Armstrong Whitley 'civilianised' bombers. These were replaced in the late autumn of 1943 by six civilian-registered de Havilland Mosquitoes. These night flights were an important diplomatic gesture of support for neutral Sweden which had two DC-3s shot down on its own service to Britain. In time, thirteen Mosquitoes were operated by BOAC, of which five crashed (not due to enemy action). The aircraft seen here is G-AGFV. (Historic Military Press)

Soon after the daylight flights started, Captain Gilbert Rae was returning in a Mosquito from Stockholm – it should be noted that the aircraft bore civil markings, clearly shown – when he was attacked by a Focke-Wulf Fw 190 at a height of about 17,000 feet. The German fighter made a cannon attack from astern, and although the speed of the Mosquito enabled it to get clear away it did not escape unharmed. The starboard wing and the fuselage were holed by cannon fire, the hydraulics were shattered, and the escape hatch was shot off, sucking everything movable from inside the cabin. Captain Rae turned back for Sweden, to make a successful belly-landing on an airfield north of Stockholm; his touch-down speed, with his wheels up and his flaps not working, was more than 120 miles an hour. The aircraft was damaged, but was before long back on service.

It was decided after that to abandon the daylight flights. The Mosquitoes were switched from day to night, and the other types of aircraft were temporarily withdrawn from the route.

When things were thus organised, the airmen were suddenly faced with a problem. There came an urgent demand from Air Ministry that two passengers should be flown to Sweden that same night; these passengers, both elderly men, were officials concerned with the ball-bearing industry, and it was essential that they should be in Stockholm the following morning to counter an enemy move designed to deprive us of that source of ball-bearings and to secure it for themselves. The importance of this mission has since been underlined by Bomber Command, which thought it well worthwhile to concentrate large attacks on the ball-bearing factories of Germany.

Now, the cabin of a Mosquito simply will not take a passenger; there is barely room for the two men of the crew. The only solution was to strap the passenger into the bomb-bay, a dark little compartment in the belly of the aircraft, reached only through the bomb-doors opening downwards and without access to the inside of the machine. This compartment is barely large enough for a man to lie down inside, and not high enough for him to sit upright. However, this was necessity.

The bomb-bays of two Mosquitoes were padded with felt and equipped with safety-belts. One passenger, muffled in flying-clothing, was pushed into each and strapped down; when the bomb doors were shut on him, he could stretch out his legs. An electric light had been hastily rigged inside the bomb-bays, and an intercommunication telephone point inserted, so that the passengers could read books and talk to their pilots on the journey. Each was given some sandwiches and a flask of coffee, and told to hope for the best. In that manner they were taken safely to Stockholm, and brought back again a few nights later, their mission successful.

The precedent having been set, passengers were soon frequently ferried between Leuchars and Stockholm in Mosquitoes in this manner. It was with a passenger Scotland-bound in his bomb-bay that Captain Rae was attacked once more by German fighters one night of bright moonlight in July 1943. Two of them intercepted him at a height of 23,000 feet over the Skagerrak. He dived violently in a series of turns to sea-level where, at full throttle, he was able gradually to pull away from the fighters.

So violent was the evasive action that Radio Officer J.S.W. Payne, thrown about the cabin, needed a fortnight to recover from his injuries. And when, the danger past, the captain tried to call the passenger on the intercommunication telephone, there was no reply; he had passed right out, and remained unconscious for some 20 minutes, though he was perfectly all right when they released him at Leuchars from his cribbed space. Captain Rae later lost his life on this service.

To demonstrate the capabilities of the Mosquitoes on this route there is the remarkable series of flights made early in 1944 by Captain J.H. White. He flew three journeys, a total of 2,400 miles, in nine flying hours, with only three-quarters of an hour on the ground meantime. He flew the whole distance by hand, on instruments at night.

CHAPTER 23

Roundabout to Russia

IT HAD AT one time been thought to extend this Scandinavian route to Russia; there were various considerations, however, which led to flights to Russia being routed non-stop from Prestwick in Scotland to Ramenskoye, an airfield some 30 miles from Moscow.

In the autumn of 1942 a crew was picked from the Atlantic service to make a survey flight of this direct route to Russia. The Soviet authorities laid down regulations for a channel for incoming aircraft passing over Riga, in Latvia, thence via Yaroslavl to the Moscow area. Captain Percy, who was placed in command of the survey – a Liberator had been detached from the North Atlantic Return Ferry for the task – worked out a route which led from Prestwick directly north to the Arctic Circle; eastwards along the Arctic Circle; a sharp dash southwards across northern Norway and Finland, and down the Gulf of Bothnia; and a turn to the east at Riga. The flying distance involved was about equal to that of an Atlantic crossing.

The Liberator took off from Prestwick on the evening of October 21st, 1942, with a crew of four, eight passengers, including officials of the Air Ministry and British Overseas Airways, freight and mail. It was desirable to reach Norway in darkness, essential that it be still dark when they passed over the Russo-German front lines, and that it be light for recognition purposes as they approached Moscow.

The outside temperature on this flight dropped to -40°, so that the crew and passengers, wearing only normal flying-kit, suffered somewhat from the cold; on later flights, electrically heated suits were provided. The bad weather for which they had hoped over Norway let them down. A bright moon shone from a cloudless sky. They travelled with some nervousness across this stretch, watching their tail-path lest they should start forming a vapour trail which would inevitably have betrayed them to any enemy fighters. But all went well; the only interference came from ill-directed anti-aircraft fire as they passed over the front lines south of Lake Ladoga.

Radio Officer D.N. Rennie, a veteran of the merchant air service – and incidentally the first British airman, as distinct from pilots, to complete one hundred Atlantic crossings – was smiling with pleasure at the help which the Russian radio men were giving from the ground. They

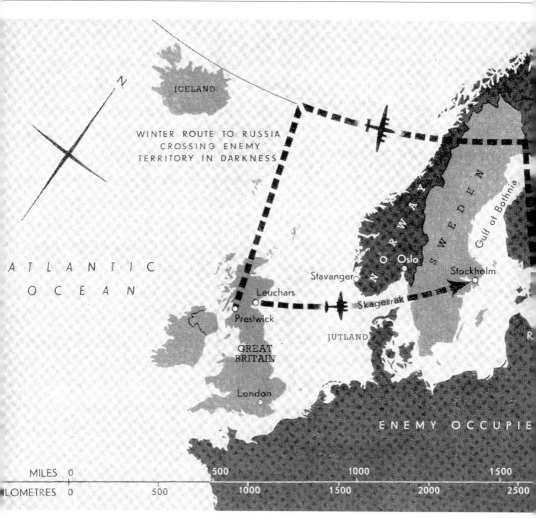

The civilian airman's route to Stockholm was straight through the enemy's fighter defences. It was flown in Mosquitoes. The route to Moscow made a wide winter detour along the Arctic circle, flew overland at night and crossed enemy-held territories at right angles. During the long Arctic daylight, the southern route through Persia was used.

dispensed with codes for the occasion and broadcast in plain English. The aircraft itself preserved strict wireless silence till morning, by which time it was travelling over the vast plains of Russia, relieved only by lonely roads and small villages, all seemingly built to the same rectangular plan.

At Ramenskoye airfield, which was then being used also by Russian bombers against an enemy still threatening Moscow herself, members of the RAF Mission stood with a number of Russian officials, awaiting the arrival of the Liberator. The Mission members were a little nervous, for

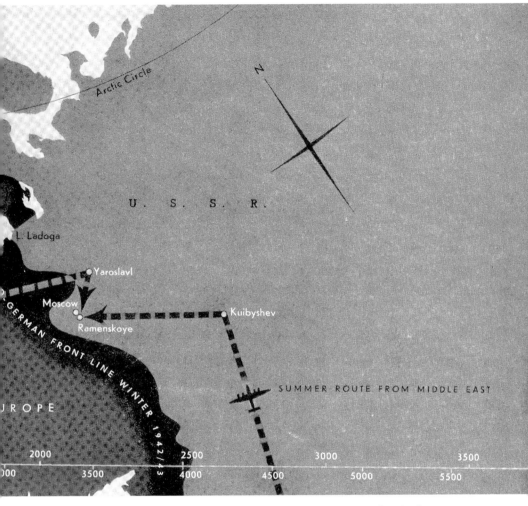

they knew in what conditions Captain Percy was making his flight over a route never before attempted. As the time which had been signalled from Prestwick as an estimate of arrival drew near, one of the officers glanced at his watch and observed to the Russians that, although the aircraft was actually due in three minutes, they must not be surprised if it were so much as a couple of hours late on such a flight. Barely had he said these words when the engines of the Liberator could be heard. Captain Percy actually landed at Ramenskoye two minutes later than the time he had given as estimate. The flight had taken 13 hours 9 minutes.

It was while preparing for the return journey that trouble started. Ramenskoye was so busy with bombers that no hangar space could be allotted to the Liberator, which had to stand out in temperatures well below zero. Periodically the crew came to start the engines to warm them up. Starting from cold in that temperature was a tremendous strain on the mechanism of the aircraft. Under that strain, a starter shaft snapped.

Percy was in despair. The engine could not be started without the shaft, and the contemplation of how long it would take for a spare part to arrive from England sickened his imagination. Then a most remarkable thing happened. A Russian mechanic who happened to be nearby, and who could speak a little English – Percy never learnt his name – asked what the trouble was, and could he help? When it had been explained to him, he brought along a few more mechanics, who started to take the shaft out – a big job on a frozen airfield without the proper tackle. The mechanic cheerfully promised to make another shaft.

At this stage the captain retired to Moscow. He was doubtful whether the Russians could get the shaft out in the first place, and quite certain they could not duplicate it; however, it was a slender hope, and there was nothing else he could do. Next day his co-pilot reported that the Russians had removed the shaft without removing the engine, in itself a difficult feat, and had borne it away, promising to arrive with a new one the following morning.

To the amazement of the British, who did not think the thing possible, they kept their promise. At 10 o'clock next morning they arrived with a new shaft which they had made, machined and hardened overnight. They put it into the engine, and it worked. Percy resolved not to touch it again until they were ready to start; all he asked was that the shaft should work just once more, to get him off the ground on his return journey.

They drove to Ramenskoye for that journey in a blizzard. Since there was no shelter, they had to buckle harness on to their passengers, who included the Ambassador, in the open; one airman tore all the finger-nails from his hand before he succeeded in fixing the straps. Then they clambered into the Liberator and, very nervously, Percy tried the engines.

The new starter-shaft worked again. They came safely back to Prestwick. In fact, that shaft worked several times, before they took it out at Prestwick and, from curiosity, subjected it to careful examination. The only fault was that the Russian mechanics had not got the hardening quite right, and in time the dogs would have worn. Otherwise the thing was perfect. The captain believes that such a feat of engineering could not have been accomplished in a single night without the proper tools in any other country in the world, and had he not witnessed it, would not have believed it could have been done in Russia either.

Throughout that winter the direct northabout air route was flown nine times in this same Liberator between Prestwick and Ramenskoye. It continued to be one of the toughest routes which the merchant airmen were asked to fly, but they maintained it without mishap. Most of these flights were made by Captains Gordon Bennett (not to be confused with Captain D.C.T. Bennett of the Atlantic) and R.B. Whitehead.

The weather was often so severe that the windows had to be sprayed with alcohol every 10 minutes in order to keep them clear enough to see through. In spite of all attempts to strike bad weather over enemy territory, the moon always seemed to shine with particular brilliance over Norway and Sweden; and as summer came along, the sun proved equally troublesome. They tried to time the flights westbound so that they should reach Norway after sunset. But often the tail-winds blew with most unnecessary vigour, and sometimes brought them to Norway with such speed that the sun still lingered in the sky; to the crew it seemed it would never set.

They carried between this country and Russia important passengers and urgent documents. They carried back from Russia, on occasion, stalwart Russians who viewed the electrically heated flying-suits with suspicion, and preferred to wrap themselves in their greatcoats, drink some vodka, and go to sleep, indifferent to the cold.

As the summer days lengthened, and night retreated altogether from those northern latitudes, the hazards from enemy action became too formidable. A new route had to be sought to Russia. That chosen was traced through Cairo and Persia. The British had been for some time already in contact with Russian airmen on the airfields around Tehran, the terminal of one of the radiating Tedder-Plan services from Cairo. The Russians granted permission for British Overseas Airways to fly trial summer flights over the whole distance to Moscow, to replace the direct northabout route.

The first aircraft to make this flight, Captain O.P. Jones, carried as passenger Mr. Maisky, the then Russian Ambassador in London, who was returning to tasks of even greater importance in his own country. Since the Germans had been driven by then from Africa, Captain Jones flew to Cairo along the direct Mediterranean route. His flight plan on the outward journey did not include a stop at Tehran. He flew from Cairo to Habbaniya near Baghdad, then northwards, skirting the Caspian Sea to the west, to Kuibyshev. Mr. Maisky, who had been the captain's idea of the perfect passenger throughout, was of great help in Kuibyshev, acting as interpreter and straightening the way. Thence they flew to Moscow. The return flight was made with a stop at Tehran.

British civil airways cover the world. An Indian soldier stands guard at the Marine Airport, Karachi, India, beneath one of the most far-reaching signposts in the world, one denoting the routes of the British civil airline, circa November 1944. (Historic Military Press)

CHAPTER 24

The Chain Complete

THE STRENGTHENING OF the air routes which followed the happier circumstances of the war after the African victories was particularly marked on the old Empire route connecting Britain with the Middle East and with India. The victories had cleared the Mediterranean skies to a reasonable degree of safety, and the supply problem which was growing ever more urgent as the North African forces moved over to Europe, was that of building up stores in India for the projected campaigns against the Japanese.

The obvious main wartime route from America to India still ran across the South Atlantic to West Africa, trans-Africa, then along the Hadhramaut coast of Arabia to Karachi. But from Britain, the West Africa detour was no longer necessary; the trunk route which would have to be strengthened ran from England, with stops at either Lisbon or Gibraltar and somewhere on the Tunisian or Tripolitanian coasts, to Cairo, then through Iraq to Karachi.

It will be recalled that, in 1942, a Liberator service between Britain and Cairo had been flown spasmodically throughout even the months of worst crisis, side by side with the aircraft of the RAF Transport Command. It was resumed in 1943 and for a time stops were made at Algiers. The view was expressed, however, by the military commanders of this American zone of war operations, that it was undesirable for non-military airmen to make stops in a battle area. This decision somewhat complicated arrangements for the route, which was continued only by flying direct from Castel Benito airfield at Tripoli, non-stop to either Gibraltar or Lisbon. The loads that could be carried were necessarily lighter, but the services could be maintained.

This same decision about merchant airmen in the battle area of North Africa also proved a considerable complication when it came to strengthening the trunk route through to India – a practical expression of the British determination to regard the fight against Japan as part of the same global war, and not to relax in endeavour until Tokyo had followed Berlin into submission.

There were really two main tasks. The first was to ferry back from India to Cairo the transport crews taking aircraft reinforcements to the Burma front. By the summer of 1943 it was anticipated that about 250 airmen a month would have to be ferried thus back to Cairo to pick up more bombers and fighters. Converted Wellington bombers, and Empire flying-boats withdrawn from the Congo reinforced the shuttle between Egypt and India.

The second task was the direct supply of India from Britain. Some 16 Sunderland flying-boats, converted from military duties, and handed to British Overseas Airways by the RAF, were placed on to the route to Cairo through the Mediterranean. The West Africa detour was dying; it was the Mediterranean that counted. Everything that could be spared had to be piled on to that route, to help get supplies through to India. The new Sunderland fleet became the mainstay. Those flying-boats were worked from Poole to Gibraltar; from Gibraltar to Djerba, an island off the east coast of Tunisia in the Gulf of Gabes, where the sponge-fishing industry is said to have originated; from Djerba to Cairo; from Cairo over the Empire route to Karachi.

Eastwards from Britain, therefore, the airmen by 1944 flew two main trunk routes in addition to the enfeebled detour through West Africa and the internal routes of the Middle East. The one was the stalwart Horseshoe Section, still moving between Durban and Calcutta with exemplary regularity. The other ran from Britain through Cairo to Karachi.

What is more, the one important link in the Empire chain which had been broken had been repaired again. Although the Japanese still held Burma, Siam, Malaya and the East Indies, the airmen of Australia had once more linked their country to India.

By doing this, those tough captains of Australia achieved one of the triumphs of this story of merchant airways in wartime. From the moment when their Empire chain had been cut, Qantas Empire Airways had hankered to re-knit it. They thought it not good enough for Australia to be connected to Britain by air only eastabout, across the Pacific, the Americas and the Atlantic. Westwards, there were only two possible routes. Long-range aircraft could fly from Western Australia across the southern waters of the Indian Ocean to East Africa; or they could strike out north-west to Ceylon. The latter was chosen. It entailed a non-stop ocean flight of more than 3,000 miles.

No long-range land-planes were available. The best, indeed the only aircraft with sufficient range which we could offer were some Catalina flying-boats, seconded from military duties with the RAF Part of their cabin space was filled with extra petrol-tanks, and into what remained could just be fitted three chairs and two canvas bunks. By this conversion it was found possible to carry 1,000 kilos of pay-load over the distance involved.

The Catalinas were flown from Britain by crews of British Overseas Airways and handed into the charge of an RAF squadron at the flying-boat station of Kegalle, in Ceylon. It might be thought the loveliest airport in the world. A long lagoon on the south coast of the island faces a shore of tropical beauty, daubed with palm-trees and the hanging richness of rare flowers. A corniche road leads to the nearby town of Galle, and on to Colombo, under the distant shadow of storybook mountains. The road runs by the huts and wayside villages of the Sinhalese, and everywhere it is crowded by those cheerful, comely brown people, men and women alike wearing long skirts and long black hair, loving rich colours, always smiling; outrigger canoes lie on golden beaches, a three-masted schooner rides at anchor in a palm-ringed bay; everything is sunshine and the southern seas.

The RAF squadron flew the first seven experimental flights in the Catalinas between Ceylon and Perth, Western Australia. But there was no attempt to set up a regular service; the flights always awaited weather forecasts in which the wind-strengths in different directions over different sections of the journey cancelled each other out for the whole flight. That often meant delays of several weeks. No passengers were carried.

In the middle of 1943 the route was handed over to British Overseas Airways, with Qantas acting as their operating agents. Captain W.H. Crowther, the Qantas pilot who had done much planning for the route, was placed in charge of the undertaking.

The first southbound Catalina service, Captain R.B. Tapp, took off from Kegalle at 01.50 hours G.M.T. on July 18th, 1943, alighting at Perth, Western Australia, after a non-stop flight of 27 hours 50 minutes. A passenger was to have been carried, but his trip was cancelled at the last moment, and the aircraft took only 52 lb. of diplomatic and troop mail. Tapp arrived at Perth with 400 gallons of fuel to spare.

The second southbound trip, on July 21st-22nd, took 28 hours 32 minutes, carrying one passenger, diplomatic mail and airgraph. The third, a week later, carried two passengers; it has since been found possible, in suitable weather, to carry three.

The Catalina is no air liner. Her quarters are cramped and her speed slow. In the early days it was necessary for the passengers to stand in a forward compartment for take-off, acting as ballast to trim the overladen flying-boat, and to remain there for some hours until sufficient petrol had been used to allow them to go aft to sit down. The only space aboard where a man can stretch his legs is the gun-deck aft, between the two big semi-spherical Perspex blisters. The noise of the two engines is harsh and does not relent. Only sandwich meals are possible on this journey of more than a day, and, with two big fuel tanks stuck in the cabin, nobody may smoke.

For the captain, navigation is the problem, for if that fails he will exhaust his fuel, and there are no alighting areas in which he can find haven in emergency. Either he navigates correctly and arrives safely, or his navigation is at fault and he does not arrive at all. So every hour he or his first officer go aft to the gun-blisters, raise them against the winds, and cast flare-bombs on to the surface of the sea, from which they can calculate their drift through the changing skies.

There was a little more speeding-up to be done. The main purpose of this Ceylon-Australia service was to carry vital official despatches with the greatest speed between London and Australia – the passengers, although important, were incidental. On the earlier flights there was a delay of three days getting the official mail from Ceylon to the north of India. To remedy this, Qantas extended their Catalina service from Ceylon direct to Karachi, in one overnight hop – the east coast of India is unsuitable for flying-boat alighting during the monsoon periods. Thus official despatches reached Karachi from Australia in two jumps, and went straight to London.

It is fitting that this account of the work of British merchant airmen during the war should end with Catalina service between Australia and Ceylon. For not only was that service a considerable feat of airmanship, it was also a symbol of the courage and endurance with which the merchant airmen have kept the air routes open despite all the difficulties and dangers of war.

The cut in the air line to Australia had been the second most serious threat to that "air empire" which a certain Herr Rosenberg had once stated in Das Reich to have "declined," and to Britain's civil air power which he had considered, in a moment of optimism, to have "collapsed." Yet with aircraft by no means the most suitable, the Australians nevertheless repaired that line across more than 3,000 miles of ocean. So that, by 1944, not only were all the countries of the British Commonwealth linked as firmly as ever through the air, not only were there new British air services to all the major allies of the United Nations, not only were merchant aircraft plying on all the supply routes to the battlefronts; but any man whose work was deemed by the Government of sufficient importance to the war could circumnavigate the globe by air, from London back to London, and travel every mile of the way, save the stretch of the Pacific between New Zealand and the western shores of the Americas, with a British merchant captain in the cockpit.

This narrative has attempted to be a plain account of the deeds of Britain's merchant airmen during the war, nothing more. Even as a plain account it is incomplete; written while the war still continues. Yet it seems unlikely that much more will have been added, by the day of publication, to the broad outline of the story. The pattern has already been drawn.

As for the future of Britain's civil aviation, that is a matter quite outside the scope of this account. Here is simply a statement of what has been done during the war years.

Yet the narrative has sadly missed its target if it has not made clear the finest of all assets which British civil aviation possesses – the merchant airmen themselves. Whatever the difficulties, they have placed themselves beyond any reproach. With equipment often obsolete, but with a spirit unbeaten and unbeatable, they have kept the air routes open at home and overseas, fair weather or foul, through peaceful skies in the back areas and through those infested with the enemy, over mountains and across vast oceans. That small group of stalwart captains who pioneered the air routes of peace over jungle, swamp and desert, flung out new routes in the midst of war, and flew sometimes where none other had dared to fly. They were joined by other, younger, equally efficient and gallant airmen as the war proceeded. They have carried the Civil Air Ensign wherever it has been demanded.

All this they did without fuss or publicity, unassumingly and cheerfully, as part of their normal tasks. It is impossible to be pessimistic of a merchant service in any future world which is manned by such as these. They have deserved well of their countries.